THE

BEAUTY WITHIN

TRAGEDY

How a Resillient Soul can turn Grief into Gifts

By: Robin Gargano

Introduction

Does anybody have a handbook for life? If you have one, please pass it along because I would love to read about how we are supposed to handle tragedy! Since I'm assuming you have never received a copy, I'm going to tell you a story of how I lived through multiple tragedies and found appreciation for the beauty within these times that led me to new happiness.

As you read through the pages, you will encounter short stories filled with lessons learned, inspiring quotes, songs, and the tools needed to heal. Each chronological story journeys through my twisty path and shows all the moments that changed my life forever: Stories of love and happiness as I found my soul mate; the death of a dream to be parents; the infiltration of a family member and the spiral it sent my marriage down; the tragic death of my husband; the second tragic death of my brother; and the fight I pursued to become a mother.

I will encourage you to find hope when it seems lost, teach you how to become best friends with grief and vulnerability, and explain why it is important. I will help you maneuver through the battlefield with a more open heart and mind because you will understand why accepting hardships are paramount for healing. You will walk away from this story feeling peace with your journey by understanding lessons I learned while walking through the storms I embraced. You will learn to have a more open mind to the realizations of why tragedies happen in your life. Then you will feel a weight being lifted from your soul when you understand why time is also your best friend, and you never should apologize for the length of your healing. You will find your voice and heart again as you venture towards new happiness.

This story is not about the small changes that occur in life. It's about the tragic, soul-sucking, and utterly depressing moments that shake our world. It's about the fight we must embrace to endure the long haul for the transformation to be fulfilled. You will read about my 'happily ever after' and how I crawled back from darkness to find a new and brighter light. The joy of this book will show how suffering is necessary to build the 2.0 version of yourself and achieve greatness. This story allows you to recognize the catalyst to happiness and provides the tools to achieve it.

I wrote this book because I now understand that there is beauty within tragedy.. My wish is to help you grieve freely, accept, transform and find the happiness you deserve. I learned that I am stronger than I ever gave myself credit because I took control and slayed my inner dragon. I will help you start healing by explaining why being kind to yourself is fundamental. I will show you how to live positively despite any circumstance thrown your way.

It's not necessary to walk the exact same path as the person next to you in order to experience the same pain. Struggle is relative to your situation and should not be compared to anything or anyone else. Walk with me as I help you accept your new life after tragedy and love all the new beginnings to come.

Dedication

To my parents who gave me the gift of a loving family.

To my 4 daughters who give me the gift of Motherhood.

To my man who everyday gives me the gifts of vulnerability, next level support and everlasting love.

To my brother who gave me the gift of him.

To my husband who gave me the gift of marriage and life lessons that changed my life.

To my family who gives me the gifts of crazy, supportive, unending love and friendship.

To my tribe of besties who gives me the gifts of fun, laughter and genuine selfless love.

To my KD sisters who give me the gift of true AOT sisterhood.

To the Rollins English department that gave me the gift of realizing my editing downfalls, accepting I don't have to be perfect in writing and the power of having a professional Editor in your corner.

To HCL 25 who gives me the gifts of authenticity, connection, belief, and bad ass leadership. Without whom this book may have sat unfinished for another 2 years...or longer!

To Dr. Mack who gives me the gift of ethical, genuine professionalism in the publication of this book along with the belief he has in me and my career.

The Beauty Within Tragedy

The Starting Point

Wow, where do I even begin with this saga? Some have referred to it as a Lifetime Movie, others a tragedy of occurrences, and some a happy ending. I refer to it as my beautiful mess.

L ife doesn't provide a handbook, road map, or warning signs. It does let us know that we are in control of our life's worth. Part of this control is acceptance of all things. Circumstances occur throughout our time on this planet, and most of the time we have no control over these moments. They happen, and then we must figure out how to deal with them. Sounds easy, right? Nope, not even close. In fact, it's a damn struggle to learn how to deal with suffering. It's a daily punch to the gut while you're trying to find air in shark-infested waters.

Acceptance will be a key topic within this book, and enacting the **3P** healing mantra, as I call it, will help you channel this understanding. Treat your journey as **Personal, Precious,** and full of **Perseverance**. The **3P's** will allow you to mold your healing and your words the way you choose. I allowed others to dictate my emotional state at one point, and not only did that set me back, but it gave way to other problems I didn't need to deal with during my journey.

Make sure you understand why your path is so personal and explain it to others who try to control your walk. Treat the journey like a precious gem. Assign it a color and think about how this stone will become the most beautiful gem you have ever laid eyes upon. Even though it may appear black now, I promise you that as time ticks forward, it will turn to your favorite and most brilliant color. Know that you will have to find Perseverance to rise and become a better you. There's a fight you will find inside of you when you decide to charge forward. This fight does not need to happen days, weeks, or months after your tragedy. You just need to be aware that to progress to happiness, Perseverance needs to prevail.

While you're swimming, which feels like drowning, you will ask yourself, *"How will I ever get back to the person I was before this happened?"* I asked myself this question daily, and although I now float in a crystal clear, aquamarine sea, there are still times a shark comes up and bites me. That bite doesn't affect me like it did when tragedy struck the first time, and that's the beauty of living and transforming through pain. Your present pain should be felt fully so the next bite will not hurt quite as much.

You will get to know your three new best friends: **Grief, Vulnerability,** and **Time.** If you don't call them friends then they will become enemies. You will get comfortable with the term grief gauge and the voice it needs to speak to the outside world. Empowerment will wash over you once these lessons sink in and you will feel encouraged to make a growth plan. The necessity of transformation will be a priority to replace stagnant negativity. You will learn how inspiration reintegrates into your world and that minor signs shouldn't go unnoticed. Through all of this, you will learn what is unnecessary and inhibiting you from moving forward.

The Beauty Within Tragedy

This is the starting point for your new life and how you can rewrite the ending. Your story will become clear, and answers understood if you walk with me through the darkness to see the light.

"One day, in retrospect, the years of struggle will strike you as the most beautiful."

Sigmund Freud

The Simple Turn

I wish I didn't take for granted the simplicity of life when I was younger. I wish I stopped to breathe in my senior year of college and didn't race to get into the real world. In retrospect I was racing because I was so excited and hopeful for my future. Through experience I understand the joy of being in the moment and why harnassing it's beauty is important. The space we are all in at a particular moment is the space we should cherish. Time is fleeting and we get to view our present as a gift. I can never go back but, I learned a valuable lesson of being present with time.

What I don't take for granted is how I came into this world. Don't worry, I won't start with sliding down the birth canal, but I will begin with the moment I first landed in my father's arms. My parents, fortunately, couldn't have kids. Weird statement to make, right? Why is that fortunate? The road was complex and tumultuous for my parents, but it led them to adoption and how my brother and I became two of the most blessed kids. We were both adopted from birth, and there has not been a day that I am not grateful to my biological parents and their selfless act. So blessed that God placed me in the lives of my amazing parents. My Mom, genuine in all her being, decided to let the nurse put me in my Dad's arms first. From what I hear, the magic of a new beginnings happened at that moment. Four years later, my brother Ryan was born, and that same magic sparked again.

The Beauty Within Tragedy

As little kids, we had a wonderful life, full of love, wonderful upbringing, genuine friends, and as many extracurriculars as we wanted (or maybe didn't want but got to try anyway). Ryan was the analytical mind, and I was the creative one; together, we built a bond like no other, and became best friends. As we got older, we spent hours defining the meaning of existence, binge movie watching, and debating about cars. We lived among the palm trees and spent summers hiking the mountains. It was and still is a great life.

High school was a challenging time. I learned so many lessons that I still enact today. Best friends that I made in high school became my family and I experienced the very first love of my life. Call it what you will, but it was the real deal to me. It was full of inexperience and puppy-dog looks, he stole my heart. Nicknamed aptly as Showboat, he was my end-all, be-all, in all facets of life. For seven years, we were on and off the rollercoaster of love, and no one could ever take his place in my head and my heart.

College came around, and boy, was this an amazing time of life! I joined a sorority and those sisters became friends I kept to this day. I had leadership roles accomplished and a degree in hand. I also was lucky in love and met the man I knew I would marry in the last semester of my senior year. Just as I was ready to jump ship and start this life I couldn't wait for, I was introduced to Nick. He was everything I wished Showboat could have been, but I saw in him what I knew I had always wanted. Genuine and full of life, Nick showed me the type of love that you read about or watched unfold on the silver screen. He made me laugh constantly, acted like a true gentleman, and we had the most fun doing nothing and everything. We were happy and a team, and we knew within two weeks of dating that this was our forever happy.

After two years of long-distance dating, Nick's job allowed him to manage his own territory remotely. So he packed up his things and we began life in the same town together. He lived with one of my best friends, which was comedy, while I was at home with my parents. As he embarked on his new job, I was in full career swing working for a boutique international PR compnay. A couple years down the road, I left my first job and started my own business. Life was happy and full until I received a strange voicemail on Valentine's Day.

The message my friend left, which I didn't listen to until the next day, asked if I had heard from Showboat. Mind you, since I met Nick we didn't speak much. We never had closure after all those years, but I accepted it as unnecessary since my heart felt completely taken care of at this point. When I called my friend back, she explained that no one had heard from him for days. I started to make some calls and was coming up short. I said something to my Mom, and then there it was"honey we aren't sure, but we think Showboat died. We didn't want to tell you on Valentine's Day." I finally got the nerve to call his Mom. I remember my voice cracking as I said hello. Before I could even ask the question, she said, "Oh honey, I have meant to come over or call you, and I just couldn't bring myself to do so." That moment stopped me in my tracks."He's gone!" It was true. I would never see him again.

I can honestly say I don't remember what his Mom and I talked about after hearing her initial statement. I think we just cried and let each other hang up. She may have said a few nice compliments about our relationship, but I can't remember what they were to save my life. My first love was gone from this Earth, and that closure I didn't think I needed slapped me right in the face.

I played our song, "You're All I Need to Get By" by the Method Man/Mary J. Blige remake, on repeat for days. I debated on whether I wanted to go to the wake. I wasn't sure I could handle seeing him lying there in a coffin. I didn't know if that vision would haunt me my whole life. Finally, the day came, and I decided I wasn't going to go. My brother came home a few hours later and told me he went to the wake; Ryan and he were extremely close. I was surprised because I didn't think he would want to put himself through that torture, but once he said it gave him some closure, I rethought my decision. He explained how I must go, so I could psychologically comprehend that he was never coming back. My brother feared that if I didn't see him, I would again not find the closure I was looking for now that he was gone. So, I called my best friend, and we went together.

As we walked into the funeral home, I felt a wave of anxiety and sadness fall upon my heart. It took me a minute to walk into the room and stand in line to pay my respects. I looked around the room as we were standing in line and locked eyes with his sister. She got up from her seat in the front row and ran to give me the biggest hug I've ever received. At that moment, I felt comfort wrapping my sadness in a warm blanket. We cried and tried to speak, but words were unnecessary. She stood with us as we got closer to the casket and then took her seat. I walked up next to the casket , and my first thought was, "How did you get here?" Followed by another thought that he didn't even look like himself, which made my heart drop. It also made me realize that his memory would live on as the free spirit I remembered and not the body that laid before me. I said a few words, prayer, and followed with the last 'I love you' I would say to his physical body.

The service was about to begin, but I decided to leave as it all became too much. As we walked out, we hugged old friends from high school and exchanged pleasantries. Finally, we made it out the front door, and my body collapsed as I fell to my knees. My best friend dropped beside me, and we just hugged and cried for what felt like ten minutes.

As I drove to Nick's apartment, I called my brother and told him he was right. It was good I went and allowed my soul to understand what this new reality was without him in the world. I pulled into the apartment complex, went upstairs, and fell into Nick's arms. He said all the right things and let me have some time on the balcony to myself. I sat there reminiscing all the years of love, drama, and lessons learned from Showboat. I cried so hard that I could barely see through my tears. I asked out loud if he could give me a sign that he was okay, in fact, I begged him. One second later, three car alarms went off in unison. The reason this is fitting is that Showboat loved cars! We had many conversations on makes, models, and the 0-60 second differential between the models. I took it as the sign I needed and immediately stopped crying, mostly from shock and because I knew he would always be by my side and he was fine.

It's been 14 years since his passing, and as life moves on and the sting becomes less, the love I felt in my heart for him remains. I still feel

19

him and know he listens when I speak to him. He made my heart full, and I will forever cherish the moments we had together. I have learned now that closure isn't always possible. But I have been able to find peace in the unresolved with him because I know our truth, and that's all I need to get by.

Thus, began how the simple turned complex and why boring started to become appealing.

Acceptance Understandings

The Unsaid. Learning to live with the unsaid will be plaguing. This process will simply take time to accept. There are times when we can't find the words or are afraid to say our true feelings. If that is the case, you will have to find a way to understand what the repercussions of the unsaid will produce in the future. If someone dies and you didn't say exactly what's on your mind, there will be struggles to overcome that void. The unsaid happens every day but be aware of those lingering thoughts that creep up behind you. They are probably expressions so strong they should be expressed.

Lessons Learned

Speaking Your Truth. This first major life shift made me rethink a few things. I know now why it's so imperative to say the things you feel are important. They may not phase someone else, but if you feel it will bring peace it needs to be said. This requires you to be vulnerable and raw, two things most are not comfortable expressing. Being vulnerable means, you trust yourself enough to know that your voice is valid and deserves to be heard. Even if the listener laughs in your face, you have the self-confidence to understand the importance of emotional expression. Try taking small steps to become vulnerable to others. You will find it opens doors to genuine friendship and closure.

Stepping into the Uncomfortable. If you are experiencing death for the first time, stop and think about how it will affect your life if you don't attend the wake or funeral. For some, this is unnecessary, but for others, it may allow your mind to compartmentalize that your loved one has been laid to rest. You may think you see your person walking down the street or mistake someone for them. This is natural. We want to see them again, and our mind plays tricks on us to fulfill this need. Remembering that they were memorialized during a ceremony can help snap your thoughts back to your new reality.

Healing Tools

Love Letters. Writing your loved one a letter is a tool that may help you release your unspoken words. If you could not say the unsaid, writing those words down will become an alternative type of closure. Speaking your thoughts out loud in private is also powerful and cathartic. It may feel unnatural or strange, but making it a part of your life cycle will become a valuable aid in your toolbox.

The Grief Gauge. This is an evaluation method I use to digest pain. I assimilate this technique with a tachometer needle on a car, but you can use anything symbolic to your world. Car enthusiasts, these terms do not reflect a proper tachometer reading or are even an accurate term, but this is my gauge. Cruise control means I am coasting through the

21

natural progression of grief. Midlining means I'm at a level of anxiety that is maintainable but creeping up on uncomfortable. Redlining is a feeling of uncontrollable emotion that may not be resolved for a long time or requires lots of inner reflection. When you can name your level of grief, you can start to figure out how to manage the emotion. Some of these emotions will be unrecognizable and will need a certain amount of attention to understand. Before we dive into the complete unknown, starting a grief gauge is a great tool to enact in your daily life. Think about what your levels of emotion may be when it comes to trauma. Use a scale and gauge them so that when you encounter a phase of grief, and there are many, you can begin the healing process by figuring out your mindset.

A Colorful Grief Gauge. Associating colors to your emotions is a visual tactic. It's also known as color psychology. As children we help teach them how to express emotions by pairing a color to a mood. This is the same tool. Typically black symbolizes the darkest point and maybe yellow signifies your balance. Find something relatable to your life. If you wake up and feel black, think of why that may be and how you can shift one thing that day to become gray or even purple. Write down a sentence that helps define your emotion. Releasing that phrase and understanding your 'black' is one perfect tool to heal, and that's enough. If you don't need to make a shift that day, simply understanding your color may make the day bearable.

This was a tactic I wish I thought of during this first life shift, but it took many years to create my gauge.

Two Became One and Added a Third

Before my first loss, my little girl dream came true. Nick got down on one knee under the moonlit sky as the waves crashed on the shore of the beach and asked me to be his wife. We drank champagne by candlelight on a blanket in the sand, and the celebrations began. The euphoria was blissful, and we felt happiness, unlike anything each of us had experienced before. We were married just over a year later, surrounded by so much love and joy. We waited to live together until after our wedding, and this was a magical decision for us. We were excited to go on our Mayan Riviera honeymoon but couldn't wait to get back and live life.

We moved into a small villa on a lake, and it was perfect for our first married chapter. Life was simple, peaceful, and it was him and me against the world. Eventually, we found a beautiful home that set us on our new journey. Settled in and fancy-free, we traveled, hung out with friends, celebrated with family, and laughter filled us both. We felt like we could take on the world together as a team, and nothing would ever break us. We rarely fought, and when we did, our communication was efficient in problem-solving. This was our happily ever after now until the day we died.

Shortly after we moved into our new home, we decided to try and have a baby. A year of trying and one submucous fibroid removal later brought no pregnancy results, so we enlisted the help of an IVF specialist. Multiple tests were run, and I was told that my 28-year-old body was behaving like a 40-year-old. My eggs had rapidly aged. We were told this news as if someone was explaining what they had for lunch that day. Shocked, I ended up in tears, and Nick couldn't find the words to express himself either.

Along with this news I understood that I had a bicornuate or heart-shaped uterus, which sounds cute, but definitely is not. This meant that it doesn't allow an embryo to grow properly due to my uterine shape potentially causing a miscarriage. Lastly, we were told that I had an excessive number of fibroids that needed to be removed.

The process of getting us ready to try for kids again seemed like a long road. I required two different surgeries to remedy my issues. The first was a myomectomy performed via a laparotomy to remove the fibroids that resided inside my uterus. Basically, that means you get cut open and cleaned out. During my 6-week recovey period, my strength was definitely tested. Next followed four months of healing before the heart-shaped laparoscopic surgery to reconstruct my uterus could take place. Finally, the second surgery was complete; more healing began and thus more waiting. Nick was terrific through them both, and we grew stronger as we ventured towards our goal. Shortly after these procedures, one of Nick's sisters graduated college and wanted to leave the cold north. We opened our home to her as she began her adult life. One big happy family appeared to take form, and the good times kept on rolling. We grew close, and I felt grateful to have a sister under my roof. The outsiders began to voice their opinion that having a roommate may not be a good idea during this time. Yet, to us, it was nice to have a full house and some distraction from frustration.

I was advised to start acupuncture, organic eating, no alcohol consumption, and stop my intense boot camp training that I loved so much. Finally, a month or so after all these changes and my new souped-up Ferrari uterus was fully healed, we were blessed with the news of a natural pregnancy! Initially shocked, Nick ran to the store to grab a new test to make sure this was real. Sure enough, it was as accurate as could be, and we screamed and cried like two little kids on Christmas morning. After all this trying, surgeries, and prayer, it was happening!

We told our best friends and found cute ways to surprise our parents with the news. Finally, all was happy in the world again, and we were going to be parents. The utter elation can't fully be explained, but we felt such relief and peace.

We counted the days until the second doctor's appointment, full of excitement and hope until we were punched in the face with bad news. Our doctor told us they found no heartbeat. How could this be happening? Our sails were full of wind, and we were soaring with anticipation of our future. The joy immediately turned to profound sadness. We left feeling defeated and exhausted. We were told I would naturally miscarry within the next couple of days. Devastated, we walked around in a black cloud for days, and I can say it was the first moment I truly experienced deep despair. Then one day, we picked ourselves up and pushed forward again, probably too quickly.

The Beauty Within Tragedy

During our first shared grief as a couple, my best friend came over for a visit. Outwardly uncomfortable, she asked if we could talk. I immediately thought she would tell me she had an illness because of how somber and nervous she was acting. As tears welled up in her eyes, she told me she was pregnant. An elation of happiness shrouded with nausea filled my body. She felt so bad that she had to tell me this news during a time of grief. I was so incredibly happy for her, even though I felt immense pain for myself. We wanted so badly to be pregnant together, and that dream seemed crushed. We hugged and talked about her first trimester. I did the absolute best I could to make her feel better and share the excitement. After she left, Nick found me in the closet laying on the floor in the fetal position balling my eyes out. The world felt beyond unfair for so many reasons. Why did I have to lose my baby? Why did her excitement have to be stifled because of my misfortune? How come we couldn't share the joy of two miracles? It just sucked, plain and simple.

Our addition wasn't a baby. Instead, it was the beginning of a unhealthy infiltration in the form of a family member, the start of the unknown and unforeseeable future.

Acceptance Understandings

Accept That Dreams Can Be Shattered. Try as you might to fight the battle you are determined to win but know that your win may be taken away. Accept the unforeseen as a speed bump and not the end. If you go into a situation looking at all the angles, you may find a better way to cope with the change you didn't expect. For example, miscarriage never crept into my mind, and that was my first mistake with this process. Some may say this outlook takes away hope. Hope will and should always remain, but when entering into territory like IVF, accepting that misfortune may occur is reality. Understanding your process entirely and communicating fears with your partner is a healthy way to comprehend potential pain.

Your Grief Does Not Stop Time. Learn to accept that your grief does not give you the right to take away joy from another. No one wants to hurt you while you're healing, but life goes on for those around us. Train your mind to have room for other moments to happen. While you're grieving, others will be celebrating, and you get to learn to accept that fact amid sadness. You can feel that things are unfair, but you do not have the right to smash the emotions of others. You do have the right to let your grief be known, and you should state that point to those in celebration if this acceptance is challenging.

Lessons Learned

Fall into Your Despair. Laying on the floor of my closet opened my eyes to the fact that I was not okay. Embrace your darkness, knowing that it is a personal journey that needs care. Do not jump up from your downfall as quickly as I did. Instead, relish in your time of sadness and be okay in that space.

Understand Miscarriages – Do not be ashamed or blameful when the worst happens. Lean on each other and protect yourselves as a couple. Men and women digest the loss of a baby very differently. Women may blame themselves because it's our bodies that couldn't hold a pregnancy. Men may feel helpless because they have no control of the situation or don't know how to comfort their wives. A miscarriage is a shared loss, shared grief, and shared healing. You don't need to feel the same emotions as your partner, but you do need to understand the validity of the other's pain. Grieving for an angel baby is personal and individual, but you can heal together by leaning on your love for one another.

Healing Tools

Survive Together. If you're a couple grieving the loss of an unborn child, share in that experience together. Do not feel that you need to battle alone. Have a conversation about how each of you would like to handle grief. Before you can help each through this process, you need to grasp how your partner metabolizes this type of pain. If one wants to be alone and the other wants to be together, work on a compromise. Understand that each one of you has lost something precious, and although you may not see eye to eye on the healing process, that's okay. Spending time alone is a good thing. because it allows our minds to work through issues without outside distraction. Spending time together gives us a sense of comfort. Speaking about your pain may provide a new perspective to your spouse and vice versa.

Walk Together. This is a great tool. Go outside and take a walk. Introducing your day with new surroundings is extremely healing. The walls of your home can carry a heavy weight when dealing with grief. Breathing fresh air and getting your body moving make you see things in a different light. Nature clears our minds and allows for simple thoughts. We all know about the happy endorphins released during exercise. Walking, even a short distance, will produce this chemical process. You may even feel a sense of gratitude for the simplistic beauty that nature provides as you breath in it's glory. Talk through your pain on these walks or pick a completely different topic to discuss. Just do it together and try to make it a habit.

Go to Therapy. Sometimes we need a third party to analyze why we feel a certain way and help us climb out of our hole. Therapy is a beautiful tool to focus on yourself or as a couple. Beginning to tackle any form of first-time grief should be met with the acknowledgment that we can't possibly understand the depths of this emotion. At this stage in our journey, we should have started therapy. We should have had a "what if" plan before our pregnancy journey and found a therapist. I will always regret that we lacked the knowledge and understanding of its importance. Why try to tread water in a pool for days or years when you can ask for a raft and make the swim more bearable? If you've never been, I will highly encourage you to go. It's like having someone read your personal biography of Chicken Soup for the Soul, analyze it, and give clarity while your sipping warm tea cloaked in a plush blanket. If you hate chicken soup, tea and blankets, then I encourage you to find a therapist.

Unlucky Number 7

I rolled over in bed one morning, and Nick said to me, "do you realize it's been 35 days since your last period?" Shocked, I told him I had no clue. The last month seemed like four, but at the same time it felt like only days had passed since our loss. I stopped cycle counting and temperature taking and just let the day's roll by. Little did I know that Nick kept track in his mind and not letting on so I wouldn't get upset or have to think about anything relating to babies.

BAM...pregnant again naturally, one month after we lost our first baby! Talk about a complete surprise and the miracle we were hoping for again. We went through such despair before learning not to take anything for granted. Beaming with excitement, we again told our family and best friends. I counted down the minutes until I could speak to my one pregnant bestie to let her know our dream of being pregnant together became a reality.

Once I told her, we screamed, and I mean screamed, with joy and started to plan our fun pregnancy things together. From the matching shirts to a possible joint baby shower, and relished in the fact that our kids would be in the same grade and hopefully be best friends like us. If you had seen the two of us, you might have thought we were delirious with how giddy we acted. It was one of the most memorable times of my life until it became the worst.

The Beauty Within Tragedy

Weeks later, the doctor told us that the embryonic sac never formed correctly, and the baby didn't make it. They called it a false pregnancy but it just felt like nails being dragged through my skin. How could anything be false about this? It felt real in the physical sense and the spiritual. In no way did we think God would have done this to us twice, especially in such a short amount of time. I had the choice of waiting weeks or possibly months until the sac naturally dissolved, or I could take a pill that would initiate a miscarriage. I couldn't bear the idea of being fake pregnant, so I opted for the second worse choice. I wonder if I would have made that choice if I had fully known what that process felt like. Six hours later, after taking that pill, I found myself on the bathroom floor curled over in agonizing pain. Cramps that felt like knives being twisted into my uterus led to needle-like pains shooting down my legs. Nick woke up and came to my side. He lifted me off the ground, and I fell into his arms from both physical and emotional pain. He walked me slowly into our home office so he could look up ideas or remedies to help ease the physical pain.

I finally took the prescription pain pill, but by that time I couldn't get ahead of the pain. He found a homeopathic drink you could make to ease the agony, so my SIL (sister-in-law) whipped it up. He also read that slow walking helped, so as he held me in his arms, we walked in circles around the house. Mostly I just had to endure this hell until it was done. I spent the next six hours curled in a nauseous ball, crying and watching as another life was stripped from my body. Nick was by my side the entire time. He was devastated for us, felt helpless and enraged that he had to watch his wife endure this pain. The following day, we went to the OB to make sure everything was clear. It was not, and I had to exist through a mini DNC procedure. Drained, lost, and physically exhausted, when it was all over we made our way back to the car and drove home. Months later, fear set in as I realized that pregnancy might not be in our future. We decided to discuss adoption. Who knew if biological children were in the cards for us? To me, adoption was a beautiful and blessed path since that is how my journey began. To Nick, it was full of anxiety regarding the unknown. After many discussions, we jumped with both feet in, or so I thought. We filled out the 37-page packet, had health physicals done for Nick, me and my SIL, and completed the home study process. We waited with anticipation and hope, knowing that this path would lead to parenthood.

Then we got the call that our study couldn't be completed since my SIL was living in our home. We were denied the chance even to be considered by potential mothers. The agency didn't feel the placement of a baby would be appropriate in a home with a young 20-something that was not our child, potentially creating an unstable environment. We couldn't believe, nor thought this would ever be a reason we couldn't adopt.

More roadblocks filled our path. Nick got up the courage to suggest that it was time for his sister to move on, although that never did happen. Frustrated and annoyed, we never told her or Nick's family the real reason why our adoption process was halted. One would think at this point, that I would have spoken up and had the difficult conversation with my SIL so we could become parents. I wish I could say I did just that, but I can't. Instead, I chose to let my husband's need to protect his sister dictate our future. This need for protection came from the loss of Nick's younger sister when he was four years old. To me it seemed his family coped with her death in a closed off manner, or at least that's how Nick portrayed things, and he had to live with the anxiety and pressure of being protective of his sister. Ultimately this was a life's mission he battled with constantly. I didn't want to add more pain to his plate by making her move out, but I ended up piling on more to mine.

I'm ashamed I didn't talk to my mother-in-law and ask for help. Help to alleviate the burden Nick placed on himself, and help to assist her daughter with finding a new home so we could move forward. I thought I was doing the right thing by protecting everyone from unspoken pain or difficult conversations. At the time, it felt like dealing with more was just too much, but I did a disservice to the entire situation. Asking for help would have given us the opportunity to have a family. It also would have helped to explain situations and paint a much clearer picture for us and the future I never expected.

Adoption was put to rest, and we decided to fully commit to the process of IVF. We hunted for a new specialist and found a group we loved. I devoted myself to getting stronger than I was at that time and kept my promise to do everything in my power to try to carry a baby to term. I started acupuncture again as both a stress reducer and IVF prep. More tests for myself and Nick were run, more waiting, and finally the first round of hormone injections. My follicles were looking great, and numbers were positively rising. Finally, the egg extraction surgery day came, and things turned out better than expected with 25 eggs to fertilize. For a uterus acting like she's 40 years old, this was great news! Of the 25 eggs, 11 were fertilized and 5 blastisized.

We chose the two best embryos for implantation and decided to have PGS or preimplantation genetic screening done. This screening allowed us to know if the embryos were classified as healthy by consisting of 46 chromosomes each. It also let us know the gender, two little girls, we couldn't be more excited! After implantation, we waited to see if I was pregnant. After five days of eating all the 'implantation food' recommended and five additional waiting days, we received the call that I was pregnant with twins! Both embryos survived. It worked! We began to feel safe during pregnancy, and that was a cherished feeling.

Extreme tiredness, hunger, and slight nausea all kicked in, and I loved every second of it. We felt invincible and understood why we needed to go down this path and have the past happen. We told ourselves that we didn't need to feel anxiety anymore because we had lost enough and now we were in great hands. We thought we could be the poster children for challenging pregnancies and help others get through their struggles. Unfortunately, as soon as we felt comfortable letting go, we received the news that one embryo had disappeared.

The doctor told us that the body has a way of rejecting something that could potentially be problematic, and for whatever reason, the PGS test didn't catch the "problem." We took a breath of sadness but were grateful we had another baby growing ever so perfectly.

The specialist stated after a couple more visits, I could be released back to my regular OBGYN. Once that time occurred, I was relieved to move on from the IVF specialist and have my first ultrasound with my OB who had been with me since I was 16. Unfortunately, Nick was traveling for work when I had the ultrasound scheduled. My Mom and I, all excited, went to the office and anxiously awaited the sound of a tiny heartbeat. We taped the ultrasound for Nick and watched a little heartbeat thump away, it was amazing and surreal, and I couldn't wait to share this excitement with my husband. Amidst the excitement, my doctor explained that the heartbeat wasn't as fast as he would like it. He told me to remain positive as my HCG levels were still high and balancing off as needed. I had a pit in my stomach as my Mom and I walked to the car. I turned to her with tears in my eyes and said I knew something was wrong. Being the supportive and loving person that she is, she tried everything in her power to make me feel better, but I just knew. Eight hours later, on Halloween night, we all sat in the ER as I lost another miracle.

Months later, IVF round two went underway as we hesitantly embarked on another hopeful path. Testing numbers were lower, as well as the number of eggs extracted. Even with this news, I became pregnant with baby number five. This time around, every day was a ball of anxiety. I tried to remain calm, rest as much as I could when not working, eat a balanced diet, and stay hydrated to keep our baby happy and healthy. One night, I woke up with flutters, which was a good sign, but also made me nervous, everything made me nervous at this point. Low and behold, bad luck hit again, and baby number five was taken from us.

Nick and I started to feel the dream of becoming parents slip away. We tried so hard to be positive, but the light was beginning to dim. Somehow, we braved enough will to try again. We were sent for more comprehensive and intense testing at a world-renown specialist, with all tests still coming back clear for Nick and myself. Although we didn't want anything negative to come back, we almost hoped for any answer regarding why this kept happening. No such luck on said answer. Round three of IVF, and this time no eggs were even fertilized. I was at work when I got the news and I remember running to the bathroom and crying in the stall. We just couldn't wrap our heads around the why.

We took a breath for the time being but started to hit a relationship wall. We weren't communicating the same. Partying with friends seemed more important than growing together, and jokes and insults were flung towards each other. I almost begged Nick to try adoption again, but I could see that his heart wasn't in it. That sent us into a deeper hole, and I started to feel like less of a woman because I couldn't give him biological children. He never quite realized the level of pain he caused by not accepting adoption as a path. So, we went back to IVF one more time, but this time using donor eggs.

The process of picking out a donor was almost numbing. I was so mad at my body for not doing what I am rightfully blessed to do, produce. We looked through the books and finally chose a great woman. As she was prepping to go through the egg extraction surgery, I also had to prep my body with injectable and oral hormones similar to the other rounds. This time, instead of feeling like a warrior who slayed her enemies that blocked her goal, I felt helpless. I cried or was mad after every injection. I couldn't understand why Nick wanted me to go through this again and blamed him for all the extra pain he was putting me through. Deep down, I know he hated seeing me like this, but he just couldn't accept another way. I learned over the years that his mental shortcomings were something I would have to accept. On we went with the journey.

A short time after that, I was pregnant with twins again. There was minimal excitement, mostly fear. We started to think maybe this was the plan all along, perhaps we just needed outside help. We prayed and hoped and hoped some more. I made it a few weeks and lost one baby. Another disappointment that seemed par for our course at this point, yet we still knew one strong baby was growing inside.

My numbers were rapidly climbing, and all seemed fine, actually more like great, and I made it to 11 weeks! We were so close to entering the second trimester, further than we ever made it before. We thought this was it, it's now our time and our miracle angel would be our fighting warrior to the end. We went in for a checkup and were preparing to hear, "we did it, we made it over the threshold and could finally take a deep breath that this was our baby, and all was going to be okay!" But our doctor had a look that was anything but happy. He explained as he held my hand that our other baby had stopped growing. Nick grabbed me in his arms as we both cried harder than we thought possible.

How in the hell was this happening again? Why, why, why? Everything felt unfair, the world was cruel, and the life was just ripped out of our souls. Since I was almost past my first trimester, I needed a DNC to remove the baby, and that was just another gut-wrenching procedure.

A month later, we went back to our specialist after he reviewed the findings of our case. He brought us into his office to express his empathy towards our situation. He had a look of genuine sorrow for the path we had gone down. He told us that we were an anomaly, and this case will go down as one that haunts him for the rest of his career. No answers or reasons for why just made this so much worse. We got in the car and sat in silence. We both felt our marriage slipping away and had no words of condolence for one another.

Our plan was wrecked, our dream crushed, and our hearts shredded. Nick and his sister became an unrecognizable pair to me, and I felt like a stranger in my own home. This misunderstood plan was never one we thought we would experience, let alone make us feel torn apart. We vowed to love each other through all of life's turmoil, and now we can't even look into each other's eyes.

We went to therapy and sat on opposite sides of the couch. Scorned and hurt, we spewed our grievances and tried to repair the damage. We both tried the best we could to unbreak ourselves and glue our team back together. We tried date nights, designed surprises for the other, and tried to get back to the fun we always use to have. We existed together but forgot to survive together. Our therapist pointed out that we never truly grieved all our losses. Instead, we just found strength to jump to the next fight without ever treating our grief as precious and worthy of the time to spend healing.

The closeness we once had was in the distance of the rearview mirror, and it was hard to love like we once did. I felt like my world was spinning out of control. I entered a realm that almost seemed like a parallel universe of disbelief. We loved each other so much for 14 years. How could things turn so dark? We began spending more and more time apart, which is when the hurt really sank deep. Then one morning, after celebrating the 4th of July, we sat down on the couch and decided to separate.

Even after those words came out of our mouths, it didn't feel real. In all truth, I think we both felt a sense of relief because we didn't have to keep fighting, fighting to grieve, fighting to fix our marriage mess, and fighting over why Nick couldn't ask his sister to move out. It was so sad and lonely, but we couldn't find the words or actions to make each other whole again. I could see that Nick gave up, and so I followed suit and did the same. The next day we went to our therapist together and told her of our decision. She explained how we were incredibly respectful of our relationship by coming in together and saying this truth aloud. Walking out of the office felt like we walked out of the life we built.

One month later, Nick moved out into an apartment with his sister. When he came to get his last belongings, we cried and hugged in the kitchen for 20 minutes. As I watched him drive away, all I could think about was how true love did an about-face in such a short amount of time? How did our strength turn into defeat? Why couldn't we find the fix? Why didn't I speak up more to his family about the issues we were having?

Why didn't I have a louder voice and make him understand? Why couldn't he love me the way he vowed and vice versa? I gave in to the fact that these questions would never be answered, and it was just best to start over no matter how weird it seemed. Little did I know, we both were entering a state of grief again, the death of a marriage.

Acceptance Understandings

Misunderstood Grief. People will not understand your grief, and you need to be be okay with this fact. Unless they walked the exact same path as you, there is no way they will internalize your pain the same. People can be sympathetic and will be for a long time, until they are not. Humans, by nature, are born to help each other. It's only later in our lives that we mess this concept up and start competing with one another. For the most part, people want to help you through your process. In the beginning, you will get all the attention and understanding, encouraging words, and gentle suggestions on how to manage your pain.

Eventually, people will get bored with your sadness and move on, that is okay too, and in fact, it's the progression of life. We all move on from something. If you can teach yourself how to accept that your grief is personal and not anyone else's business, you will manage the negative comments that come. I promise there will be negativity and some of the most shocking statements you have ever heard. But, brace for them and brush everything off that is not necessary to you. Walk your journey without making excuses for it.

Your Plans Mean Nothing. Making a plan is great but learning how to digest the change of plans is the hard part. Go into your goals with passion and hope, knowing that there may be a time when the plan is completely messed up. While riding a roller coaster, you have no control over your twists and turns, and this is also the case with life. You get to learn how to bend with the alternative. If you can't grasp this concept, you will always be in a car that someone else is driving.

Understand Outside Advice. Listen more openly and digest advice from friends and family, even if you disagree with that adice or suggestion. Those outside of our inner circle see things we cannot because we can either be naive to people we love or make excuses for things we really know aren't good. If I understood why having a family member live with us would bring us as much heartache as it did, if I would have listened to their advice and found a voice to change the dynamic, maybe things would have been different. No matter how much I loved my Siser-in-Law and how hard a conversation would have been, it also would have been the right thing to do for our family.

Relationship Kindness. Treat your relationship with kindness and respect. Respect that marriage or partnership is meant to be between two people and not shared with anyone. Being accommodating to others can backfire, so be aware of the team you want to create as a couple and stick to that plan. The two of you come first always, there are no exceptions.

Change, Changes Everything. Love changes when reality doesn't match your dreams. Love changes in many more ways than this, but if you find yourself on the same battlefield as I was, your dream may need to have a plan B. Meaning that Nick and I should have discussed our stopping point when trying to conceive. It should have been stated from the beginning that if X happens, we will agree to Y. When going through any obstacle, love should be the balancing force of why you're going through it in the first place. Your shattered dreams can ruin your relationship if you don't fully comprehend the black hole unfulfillment creates.

Lessons Learned

Do Not Hide Your Hurt. Shying away from your emotional state will only do damage to your healing. We feel wearing the mask of strength is necessary because society has bred us to believe that weakness is a negative trait. Embracing our shortcomings is a powerful attribute. Owning the sadness surrounding your world acknowledges that suffering exists and is meant to be lived through, not sidestepped. Faking happiness is even worse than living in sadness. If you are constantly hiding behind a façade, you are suffocating your chance to learn and choking your opportunity to live.

Grieve Every Loss as if it's the Only Loss Experienced. Because we never made it to our second trimester, we would get comments such as, "well, at least you weren't so far in," or "must be a blessing not to have lost your babies later." Yes, those are blessings that are now accepted, but those comments made us feel that we didn't deserve the right to grieve. That's unfair treatment from outsiders. The size of the tragedy does not determine grief; it's determined by the weight of your love and the hole that's left behind. Being strong and

43

moving on is essential when starting fresh but compartmentalizing your loss to pursue the next course is damaging. If you're not patient with your mourning and respect it for what it means to your life, it will come back and bite you hard later. To this day, I still have not grieved the loss of all my babies fully. I have had to go back and revisit this pain, strip it down and live through the moments all over again.

Make Your Voice Heard. Do not constantly fight for something that is damaging your soul. You get to take care of yourself and self-preserve. If someone's wishes are blinding their ability to see your pain, you get to open their eyes. Speak up when there are problems and ask for help from others. It doesn't matter if you seem desperate or lost. What matters is that you open your mouth and make your values important to those around you. I kept quiet on many things because I didn't want to hurt my husband's feelings or make his pain more poignant. I didn't ask my mother-in-law for help when drastic changes occurred. I didn't say that I needed her to be the voice of reason and ask her daughter to move out. If you don't validate your emotions as worthy, neither will anyone else. For all they know, things are fine because you have failed yourself and didn't trust your gut. This is one huge regret I will always carry with me. I thought I could handle it all and make it better, but ultimately, I created more damage. My display of strength even caused others to be less understanding.

Stand Your Ground. When your gut speaks and you feel completely adamancy towards a subject, do not back down. The views of our partner can be clouded by love, anxiety, pressure so to ensure you find a common groud, you get to stand for what you know is right. If your partner can't muster up the gumption to say what is right, ask if you can step in as a voice to aid the process. Communicate why you feel so strongly and find a resolution that if fitting to the problem.

When we choose to ignore our convictions it's mostly because, we are trying to be selfless towards our loved one and obey their wishes. You can find an opportunity for mutual happiness in an uncomfortable time, but there is an openness required for such growth. Over my lifetime, I have constantly learned this lesson, and it is only now that I stick up for my convictions the way I always should have done in the past.

Listen to the Professional. Take advice from trained psychologists, even if you think you know better. When Nick and I decided to separate, our therapist told us to commit to a proper separation and give it a few months. We only listened to a quarter of this advice, and I know now how stupid we were for not trusting her competence on this matter. When you go through something new and challenging, you aren't always in your right frame of mind. You think and act differently, say strange things, and feel emotions never known. Understand that you don't know it all, and there is a reason a professional is telling you to go down a different road. Trust the process.

Healing Tools

For Miscarriage. This is an extremely personal path, but in my experience, the number one tool is to give yourself time. Time to process, feel depressed, cry, scream and grieve the loss of a dream you so desperately desired. Another tool is to write a letter to your unborn child or children. My therapist suggested this, and I see how this can bring closure to a nontangible being. I started this letter many times and felt the finality of what this letter would carry. It's been five years since my last miscarriage, and I choose to write my letter for this book. Case in point, this is my new reality, and I will forever be learning how to manage it, as will you. If you are open to learning from your emotions, you are progressing to a better place.

Miscarriage: Give Your Child a Name. It doesn't matter if you were pregnant for 5 minutes or 5 months, a name can solidify that your baby was real. This may be too hard for some as remaining nameless can separate just how personal your loss becomes. If you are struggling or have been shamed by someone who recklessly stated that your grief should be minimal because you weren't pregnant for long, this tool may help you bond with the fact that you did lose a real being created through love.

Read a Book on How to Grieve a Marriage. At the time, I didn't know grief assimilated to anything else but death. I never stopped to think of all the things in life we can grieve and never learn to mourn. However, once I read all the nuances attached to the death of your love, I began to understand why it was necessary to grieve. There are many books on this topic, but you must find one that speaks to you the most.

List Things that Cannot Be Changed. Seeing occurrences on paper that took place for no other reason than it was just a part of life takes the pressure off any sense that you could have changed the outcome. Give your mind a break from overanalyzing and cut yourself some slack from blame. We feel the need to blame ourselves for so many things, be it a self-deprecating attribute or some emotional void we need to be filled, but it is counterproductive. If you make a list of items in your control, you will begin to see why situations needed to happen the way they did...and it has nothing to do with you.

List of Things Done Differently. After the initial cloud of dust has passed from your struggle, the view of your actions becomes more apparent. This could take months or even years. Write down all the changes you would make and why. Use this list as a blueprint when framing your new beginning. It will be a long-running list of lessons for review as time ticks on. Add to it and continue to grow from your missteps, always remembering they were necessary to propel creation into your life.

List of Misunderstandings. I know it's a lot of lists, but you'll see why this one is important. Start a list of the things you don't understand that occur in life and then pack it away. Do not dwell on in or reread it. Place it in a spot that you don't frequent every day. If a new misunderstanding arises, add it to the list, but put it back right after you've written it down. The day will come when you know it's time to bring out the list of misunderstandings.

The Beauty Within Tragedy

Numbness

L earning how to start over and create a new life without my husband was such a strange feeling. It almost felt like every day was fake, and I was living in a cloud of confusion. I didn't want to tell anyone the news of our separation as I couldn't believe it was happening. If I said it aloud, it became real, and I didn't want to acknowledge this reality. My identity changed, my thoughts shifted, and I felt that the fairy tale we all dream of was nothing but a lie. When close friends finally found out and asked if this was happening, my reply was, "probably not."

Through the next four months, Nick and I respected each other, or so I thought. We discussed not using social media to harm each other, and that words said to friends would remain respectful. We even shared thoughts of sadness through texts or calls as the hurt of our separation grew. Something inside us knew this was wrong, but we still couldn't seem to claw our way out of the quicksand. We sat in the lawyer's office to sign a marital separation agreement. I will never forget how we both stopped signing, looked at each other, and cried, asking if this was the right thing to do. Then and there, I should have said that we need to wait on this and examine why we feel this way. Another time when I should have spoken up about my feelings. The lawyer stated she had never seen a couple act this way, and we should take a step back, but we didn't. We left the office still crying and hugged outside.

He would drive to my work, and we would sit in his car talking. One-time, tears welled up in his eyes, and he told me he was seeing someone. We both cried, and he admitted that he had no clue what he was doing and added some words of unimportance to the state of his new relationship.

It was the month of October, and I was about to embark on an extensive work trip. We had talked before this trip and decided to meet when I came back. My trip came and went, and we agreed to meet to talk a few things out. We discussed our life together, how we got to this place, why we didn't halt our IVF journey sooner, and the regrets we both had during our downfall. My last question to him was, "why did you pick your sister over me?" A look of shock came over his face, and he immediately began to cry. He acted like he never knew I felt this way, even though we had many conversations about asking her to move out. He said, "I would never do that to you. I would never pick one person over you," and I replied with, "you absolutely did."

I can't tell you the realization he had at that moment, and I could see it all over his face. It was like I slapped him with news he never heard before. Even though I loved my SIL to a fault, I knew, besides the losses of our babies, she was a big reason we lost ourselves. He explained how he thought he was doing good by her, which he was, but to the detriment of our marriage. A couple is meant to be two people navigating the waves together, not having a third influence to weigh in on all topics or be present at almost everything we did. He never saw it, never noticed how different our lives became when she entered our home. She was our family, and he needed to protect her at all costs so he wouldn't lose her like he did his baby sister. I pointed out how his anxiety stems from this relationship. One time before she moved in he had a full-blown panic attack due to the pressure of keeping her safe. This was a constant battle and one he didn't understand until this moment. We ended our talk and left, both a bit bruised by our time together.

A couple of weeks went by and I received a text from him saying, "I can't stop thinking about what you said. I'm so sorry for what I did to you and never intended to make you feel that way. You are my wife, and I would never pick someone else over you. I'm so sorry." I pulled off to the side of the road to fully grasp what I read. I knew him so well that I believed he pondered this thought since we talked. His heart was always genuine and honest, especially with me. I felt a sense of relief that my voice was heard, and he understood the pain and damage another person caused us. He was about to get on a plane for work and said he would touch base with me after landing. We spoke on the phone later, and the tone of the conversation felt as if a shift had occured and we might remedy our issues when he returned. Relief, hope, and a million thoughts raced in my head.

The next day I received a text from my SIL's boyfriend asking me to come over to the apartment. Since we were all still friends, I thought nothing of it. I felt a little under the weather and explained that to him, but he still asked if I would please come. So I got in my car, and as I was driving, I began to feel a rush of heat go through my body, and intense worry crept in. I called Nick, and it went straight to voicemail, so I tried again, and the same thing.

The Beauty Within Tragedy

My parents texted asking what I was doing, and I told them I was on my way to Nick's apartment. As I parked and walked up to the door, my parents came running up. I asked them what happened, and they said they heard on the radio a plane had crashed in Ohio where Nick was traveling. I lost my mind and fell to the ground as SIL's boyfriend came to open the complex door. They all picked me up off the ground, and we walked to the apartment. As we were riding the elevator, I asked what happened, and my SIL's boyfriend said the plane was supposed to land four hours ago, and no one has heard from Nick.

We get inside, and SIL and I hugged and cried while trying to catch our breath. We began calling the Akron police, hospitals, and the executive aviation airport but no one could tell us anything. We asked if they could confirm who was on the manifest and why can't we get any answers to any questions. We waited, and I prayed harder than I ever prayed before. Impatiently waiting, I spoke to my mother-in-law and did anything to keep hopeful. Finally, I said to my Mom, "I have to go to work and close out some projects in case our fear is true." What a crazy thing to think, right? I believe I needed to physically do something, so I didn't spin out of control. Mom drove me to work, and after about 45 minutes of closing things out, we heard the most devastating news of my life.

The plane had crashed upon landing, smashing into an empty apartment complex on the last leg of their trip . We raced back to the apartment and thus began the worst emotional and mental torture. I spent the night in the apartment, and around 6:00 am, I crept into Nick's bed. Feeling indescribable emotions, I knew it was time to let my best friends know what happened before they heard it on the news.

Screams, crying, and pain filled our conversation and every conversation with every person I knew for weeks. I thought the first day I dealt with his loss would be the worst, but I couldn't have been more wrong. Friends and family gathered, and utter shock set in, inhabiting my being for a long time.

I wasn't hungry or tired, although my body was exhausted, and my mind was paralyzed. Food wasn't even on my radar, and my Italian self loves food. But I only ate to merely survive. When I did sleep, my body passed out unaware of trying to fall asleep. That first week, I sat on my parent's couch, barely moving or thinking. I couldn't turn on the TV because every station, or it seemed, showed pictures of the fiery crash, which sent my body into physical pain. Photos of the crash were posted on Facebook, and I screamed, asking people to take them down. I went crazy. As the days followed, I couldn't speak properly; words were hard to find within my vocabulary, even simple words used every day. I couldn't understand things or comprehend anything. I was numb. Drastically depressed, extraordinarily underweight,I had no care about what was happening in the outside world. My family and friends were amazing. They carried me on their backs and helped me survive.

If we call this tragedy the tsunami, the tornado followed quickly thereafter. I will condense the next portion of the story so I don't give life to what I now deem unnecessary. There are a million details of this tornado, but a summary version is vital to understand what brought me healing. Lines of communication between mine and Nick's family began to get crossed. Actions were deemed manipulative, and words carried vindication while viewpoints were unseen. My family tried to take on the bulk of responsibility with Nick's burial arrangements to unburden the plates of others. Misunderstanding of intent sank in and bit us all harder than we could have imagined. I'm sure my in-laws thought they were acting appropriately.

Grief makes people go into a state of altered personality. Shock ends up protecting us from the initial trauma, but it makes us transform into a version of ourselves we don't recognize. That is what happened on both sides of our fences. Instead of loving each other through this process, I was the evil, almost divorced wife who left their son. My family was to blame for anything that didn't run smoothly. Rumors turned to lies, and my whole family became outsiders to Nick's life. How could 14 years of life together as a family unit be erased by four months of separation?

There was a funeral in New York, where he was from that me, my parents and best friends attended. You would assume this would be an awful experience, but the word awful doesn't even come close to describing it. By this time, my SIL, mother-in-law, and I were not speaking. I got a firsthand taste of friends pulling away and felt shunned by those I once shared great times. The wake was the most somber and maddening moment of my life. Picture walking up to your love's wake thinking about what could have been when he returned from his trip, feeling like a mac truck keeps running over you, and seeing pictures of his rebound chick in print and in a slideshow.

Nick looked unrecognizable in their pictures; his smile wasn't the same, his eyes weren't full of life, yet people believed he was happy. To me, it was so blatant that unhappiness was written all over him. Follow this by his rebound chick at the wake, referring to herself as his girlfriend. Between my scathing, it took everything in me not to laugh as the night before he died, we talked of reconciliation. But who would believe me now, and what business is it of anyone? The saving grace of that evening was one of Nick's relatives kept introducing me to strangers as his wife, and for some reason, it was that small gesture that validated who I was in this room. I was a frail mess and had no strength to know my place in this moment, but the hits just kept coming.

The funeral was the next atrocious, awful experience. It felt like nothing of him and who he was to this world was included in the funeral. The turnout of people was beautiful, but the ceremony was traditional and stiff, nothing what we discussed as last wishes for each other. A hundred things made this unbearable, but the moment I saw the "rebound" get up from the pew and become a participant in his funeral is when hell entered this church. I turned to my best friends in complete shock and asked, "What was going on?" My friends were in awe, and we all balled at the manipulation of events as we knew how Nick felt about this woman.

The glare I received from her as she took her seat was full of entitlement and disrespect. It showed us all who she was as a person. I don't even have a word to describe this next event; my body started shaking from head to toe, and I couldn't control it or stop it. My friends wrapped their arms around me and held my legs to try and bring me back to a state of calm. But the force of disbelief that Nick was gone and the shock that my SIL made this act happen was beyond overwhelming. This service couldn't end quickly enough, and when it did, I almost ran out of the church. I felt stripped of my time to accept what was happening around me. I saw evil for the first time. We all skipped going to the cemetery and the party afterward to try and find a tiny shred of peace.

From that moment on, I started to hear rumors from friends, some stopped talking to me, and others slandered my name. Complete lies were told, and then I began to realize the man I loved didn't keep his promise. To the outside world, he was happy-go-lucky and moving on with his life. I heard statements from people saying, "He had never been so happy." This statement proved to me that Nick found a great way to move on, act stronger than he was, and lie about his happiness while breaking his promise of respect towards me. I was asked if I knew about the rebound, another blow to the chest that sparked mini twisters amongst the tornado. Of course, I knew, he told me, we spoke all the time about us, but he never told anyone else of this truth. How could he do this? I trusted what we said to each other and didn't utter one negative word about him. How could he leave this world and have me pick up pieces that my now ex-friends believed to be true? For years this went on and every time it chipped away at my soul.

I finally came to realize that Nick wasn't strong enough to handle the truth of our defeat. He needed to put on this façade to survive. I say this not to be mean, but to be real. I knew of his suffering, and it took me a long time to understand that we all need to protect ourselves the best way we can. I was mad for so long but loved him so much. I don't blame him for acting this way, and I accept why it was done. I am by no means perfect and acted in ways that were unbecoming, but I kept true to my word. The conflicting emotions and outside voices made my grief worse than it needed to be. I wished we never separated first and foremost, but also wished I could grieve normally and without backlash from people that had no idea what was going on. Not only was I losing the love of my life, I lost friends, extended family, and the future I thought would unite us back together.

I'm praying for the winds to mellow and the rain to stop, but the earthquake was next. It could have been weeks after the funeral, to be honest I can't remember, when I received the dreaded envelope. I was being petitioned by my mother-in-law. I could write an entire book on how I became a lawyer by osmosis during this process, but it's not worth it. She didn't feel I was entitled to anything of Nick's and made that known. A woman that I called "Mom" took her pain and stabbed me in the back with a rusty dagger.

I still have a hard time understanding why someone wants to add more stress to an already horrific situation, but that's what happened. Living through grief and adding the pressure of a legal battle sucked the life out of every fiber of my being. My physical breath was shortened, and my heartbeat felt heavy every day for eight months. That eight months wasn't even the end as the NTSB legal battle lasted for years. Ultimately everything was settled peacefully, and I now understand why this had to happen between us. Her pain of losing another child was unbearable, and the horror was magnified. I was the person to blame, the one to cast all that unfair darkness. Having not walked in her shoes, I can't possibly understand the pain associated with surviving two children. No parent should have to endure that type of cruelty and suffering. My wish for that time was to be in grief together, loving each other through the pain. We could have eliminated despair if anger didn't cloud our judgment. More love could have been shared if understanding was an option. More time for preservation could have happened if swords were laid down and hearts opened.

The beauty that came from this time was I learned how to accept another's pain. I understand that actions, although unwarranted and unnecessary, are a part of the life cycle. This proved to me how pain can be used for the betterment of self or self-destruction; how it uses you or you use it. Pain and suffering can be used positively. It didn't matter how unfair, but what mattered was who stuck by my side, who helped me achieve resolution. What mattered was that I found peace to live and move beyond something that destroyed me. As time passed, apologies, hugs, and tears made it all settle in a place of comfort.

I tried to go back to work only three short weeks after the accident. I thought keeping my mind busy would be good for my soul and a chance to escape such sadness. Try as I may, I failed at my return. I worked for a wonderful company that had supported me through some of my worst life moments. So, I wanted to be back and help my team, but ultimately, I was a hindrance, making mistakes and oversights I would never have missed prior. I would look at a computer screen and reread emails five times. I couldn't process standard contracts that I read a hundred times before. I would just stare at a screen full of words a few times, and it just looked blank, like a bare Word document, and I couldn't focus to see anything for a few minutes.

At this point, I knew I was in a state of trauma and needed to walk away for the sake of my team and, most importantly, my mental and physical health. So, I gracefully resigned with the most heartfelt sentiments from my entire team and business unit President and walked into a new stage of life. I was truly afraid of this new stage and had no way of knowing how I would feel or how to deal with healing. In the past I was never scared of the unknown. In fact, I relished in possibility and the excitement that it would bring. But this was the kind of unknown I had no clue how to maneuver, and it seemed daunting, frustrating, and a battle I didn't want to fight.

The Beauty Within Tragedy

A Beautiful Year of Tragedy

I never thought I would refer to the worst year of my life as one of beauty. But I can now proudly say that I walked so deep into the storm and learned how to clear the skies to see the sunshine that I can now describe that year as beautiful.

This chapter is going to focus primarily on what I learned and how I lived and worked through my struggles. Hopefully, these tools will help guide you through some part of your journey. There is no exact science I can script, simply thoughts on how you can break from numbness and monotony to begin to feel like an improved version of yourself. You will forever be changed and impacted by your trauma, but there are ways to use that change positively to allow for future strength and greatness. The first step is to understand what you need to accept. Something happened to you that will always be a part of your life and story, but it can propel you into a version of yourself you never knew existed versus dragging you down through the dirt. This chapter will help you open your mind to allow for a new life, living through your tragedy instead of in your tragedy.

Acceptance Understandings

Grief is natural, normal, and necessary and is not a steady upward progression. Learn to accept what is to live fully.

Blindsided During Times of Grief Inexperience. If you have never gone through a tragic loss, you are flying blind with your emotions, words, thoughts, and actions; you are grief inexperienced. You do not know how you're going to feel from day to day and the same goes for others suffering from that same loss. When the blindsided moments occur, there's a good chance you won't be able to fix them. You are going through your own path of recovery that will be completely different from others. Accept that you can't change the viewpoint of others, even if it's a family member. They will have their account of the situation, and you will have yours.

Trying to solve issues in the midst of hurt is almost impossible because you can't relate to how others are processing. Grief is expressed in so many different ways: sadness, pain, anger, depression, numbness, love, social interaction, verbalization, or total silence. The point is these blindsides are going to hurt like hell but let them go. You have enough to deal with in your own healing journey, so worrying about what someone else is feeling is truly pointless. That may sound selfish, but it's necessary for self-preservation, and if there's ever a time to be selfish, this is most definitely it.

It's OKAY to Not Get Out of Bed. There are going to be days when your head feels like a 50lb weight; your body trembles in pain as if you ran a 26-mile marathon and your heart feels like it's ripping right down the middle. There will be days your eyes are swollen shut from crying, and your stomach is full even though you haven't eaten a thing. And even days you have no thoughts, or the ones that do creep in are horrific images of your tragedy that start your "I don't want to get out of bed" cycle all over again. Just live through them.

In the beginning stage of grief, this might be a string of days. Give yourself several days to just lay and be still. Watch TV, read, listen to music, eat anything, and sleep. Remember that your body is recovering from psychological and emotional trauma. Like any physical wound that needs time to heal, so does your mental health. Accept that fact, you deserve time, and that time might be spent in bed or on the couch. What you want to try and avoid is spending weeks living in this state. If you do find yourself repeating long spans of repetitive stillness, start a simple daily goal list. Pick a number of days to allow yourself complete solidarity of stillness, but once those days have passed, set one goal to reset your body. This can be as simple as, "Tomorrow, I'm going to sit outside for 20 minutes." Once you reach that goal, start setting another, "Tomorrow I will go on a walk." The goals you choose do not have to be monumental. They just have to be different actions that will eventually break you from that numbness. Think of things that made you happy before and apply them to your daily goal list.

As time ticks on, these days will happen randomly. You can have a perfectly fine day or even a day that made you feel like you are beginning to feel more like yourself. Then BAM, you wake up the next morning as if your tragedy just happened yesterday. My best advice for these times is to live through the day. Our subconscious plays into our daily lives more than we realize, as does silent stress. So just accept these days will come and either cry when you need to, punch a pillow or sleep it away. Yes, you can try and set a goal and try to achieve it on these days, but in my personal experience it is best not to pressure yourself. I have lived through enough to know that tomorrow you may feel different, and for whatever reason your mind may need a vacation.

Don't analyze or beat yourself up because you were feeling better, and now need to take a step back. In fact, I use to look at those days as taking a step back, but they are a huge step forward in reality. Why? Because it's natural to go through things you can't explain, it's all a part of growing. Accept when you're weak. It's a version and the presence of strength. Be vulnerable so you can understand your pain and become stronger by overcoming it. Each lousy day goes into a vault of data colleciont for observation on why they are occurring. Is it the anniversary of something, a birthday, or a suppressed memory? You may not know the answer in the beginning, but eventually, you will go back to your grief gauge and know that when X time comes around, you're potentially going to be numb.

Living through weakness helps educate the mind. When you learn how to ride a bike, your mind is being trained on the steps you take to achieve the goal. This same methodology goes along with pain. When we feel emoitoanl pain, our brain learns how to cope. The only way we learn how to cope is by practicing how to accept and understand our pain. If we suppress it, our mind will never understand how to move forward in a healthy way. Supression allows us to accept that pain should be masked and not felt. By examining why we feel something, we allow that "something" to teach us a lesson. A lesson in healing, self-preservation, resiliency, strength and we give ourselves the gift that feeling emoitons and speaking about them is a good thing versus a weak thing. I personally find it rather weak when someone denies themselves the gift of self-revelation.

People will Not Understand Your Pain. It's okay if people don't understand your pain. Trying to explain your pain should never be met with opposition, but sometimes this is the case. You know that saying "let their words run off your back?" Make that your mantra when dealing with someone who thinks they know what's best for you. If someone hasn't walked exactly in your footsteps and vise versus, there is no way they can measure your pain or understand your process. It's also none of their business what your process is and how long it takes you to feel differently about your grief. I felt at times it was my responsibility to make others understand my depression because I was met with some shocking comments, such as "I think you have an eating disorder," or "when do you think your depression will be over?"

People sometimes say things because they don't understand or are uncomfortable with grief. Typically, those individuals either suppress pain or have not lived through something that has changed their whole world. You are dealing with something that is very personal so when you're met with unsolicited and sometimes rude comments, try to have a line prepared in response. This was something I learned to arm myself with as these comments would come from all angles, mostly not even being prompted by any related discussion. My response was, "my journey is a lesson I will learn from whether or not you understand it." It was such a broad statement that I rarely got any response except a head nod of understanding that we will no longer discuss this topic. If you don't want to address things, just let those words run right off your back and disregard the ignorance.

Time Does Not Heal All Wounds. I grew up hearing the phrase "time heals all wounds" over and over again, but I learned it doesn't ring true for every circumstance. The wounds that run deep will never heal; they will simply manifest themselves into whatever you make of them. Could you possibly ever heal completely from losing a person that was your whole world or never getting to meet the child that was growing inside of you? You can't, but you can learn how to make those moments mean something beyond what they are.

The saying should go, "time will transform the wounds." These wounds become a part of your being. Time transforms your thoughts, your outlook on life and people, and changes the way you handle a variety of circumstances. In the early stages of grief, you're so clouded because there is no making sense of what just happened to your world. You feel emotions that have never surfaced before and go down a path so uncharted you can't see what's ahead. But, as time moves forward, so do you at your own pace. The clouds become less dense, turn from black to white, and you do see clear skies again.

If you think of your pain as a lifelong teacher rather than a moment you wish was fleeting, it will become palatable. Pain can be positive if you accept the challenge to make it that way. One does not wake up one day feeling all the better from trauma like recovering from a cold. Instead, you learn how to find a new harmony and a balance, especially when the grey clouds come rolling in again. Your grief will surface throughout your life, so accepting that time as a transformer rather than a healer can change your outlook on how to live within a new reality.

You Get to Learn Patience. I remember thinking that I wish this would all just be over and I could get on with a new normal life. I was so mad that I couldn't speed up the healing process, and I longed for years to pass at warp speed. But, of course, they didn't, and I had to remind myself that patience is a virtue. I either had to accept that time moves on as it's supposed to and my journey would take time to understand, or I would have to accept suppressing every emotion I was having, never dealing with the pain, and live a pretty unhealthy life. Even though those days were some of the most difficult ones to endure, I'm so proud that I had the guts to accept myself and value my worth while giving myself the gift of patience during such a negative period.

No matter how long it takes, the lengths you have to go, or the tests you give yourself, it's all worth it if you believe you can survive beyond your pain. The darkness I felt made me question so many things, but there was always a tiny voice inside that said, "You know you can do this. You are meant to live again." All I needed was that little voice pushing me a step forward to accept being patient of time because I was worth it.

"One day, in retrospect, the years of struggle will strike you as the most beautiful." – **Sigmund Freud**

I came across this quote about nine months after I lost Nick. I didn't take for granted that it resonated so much more fully now than it would have if I read it a year prior. Almost six years later, there is nothing I believe to be more authentic than this quote. That entire year was full of multiple struggles that burnt me to the core, but now I look back and see how each struggle repurposed so many aspects of my life. I let my voice that I silenced at times, be heard unapologetically loud and clear. I celebrate simplicity and yet encourage abundance. I now withhold giving trust unless it's earned versus giving the benefit of the doubt. I know what is most valuable to hold on to and where I never want to return.

But the most valuable beauty lesson is that nothing can change the outcome of the tragedy, but the unexpected gifts it gave me were beyond anything I could have dreamed. The lesson of understanding that my past life gave birth to my new one was almost surreal and oddly inspiring. Those struggles and the ones that I still have to deal with today are all moments that enlighten my mind and widen my understanding of vulnerability. That time was full of reflection that provided a great relationship with vulnerability. I can be happy with my rawest self and share stories that may make others uncomfortable but hopefully help someone who needs to hear them.

I am grateful that I can now call this time some of the most beautiful years. You may not believe that is possible for yourself, but it is achievable if you trust in the process, keep your mind open to everything and work on healing yourself.

There Will Be Triggers. You will be triggered by many things along your journey: a song, a TV show, walking into a place that was a familiar hang out, smells, etc. Expect them and take a deep breath when they occur or cry if the emotion is overwhelming. The only way I was able to feel better in those instances was to try and recall a good memory to replace the sadness of the trigger. The first year this is hard, because mostly what you feel is sadness and there aren't any memories that seem to come to mind when you need them.

I felt stuck trying to recall things that happened, almost like I forgot my life, which was terrifying. So, during regular times I would write down some of my most fantastic memories with Nick, and when a trigger happened, I would whip out the list and read through them. Sometimes it helped and other times it didn't, but you have to remember that these are all tools to try and help you. Whether they always work or not isn't important. The important part is you are trying to learn how to adjust your life in that person's absence.

You will also be triggered by shadow grief things such as anniversaries, holidays, birthdays, and special occasions that can causes a downward spiral. I knew I would be sad when these occasions came around, but I didn't anticipate how leading up to these moments would transform me without notice. In the first couple of years, you can imagine the emotion related to these times, but as the years pass, you may think you are better at handling them when in reality, they have found a way to be subconsciously prevalent.

Meaning, I have found that the week prior to, what used to be a special time, my body starts to feel sluggish and more annoyed with things and people around me. I'm shorter with my responses, and I don't sleep as well. My anxiety rises, but not in an overwhelming way. It's duller yet present throughout the day. Then when the actual anniversary day would hit, I would cry just as if I lost Nick yesterday.

The Beauty Within Tragedy

It took me a few times to go through this shadow grief before I could figure out how to help myself. I have asked someone very close to me to be my human reminder one week before the times that trigger me the most. This person knows to remind me of what is coming gently so I give myself a break during that week. I thought of setting an alarm to remind myself, but there is something about invoking the help of loved ones that makes these times bearable. You can't recover all on your own, you do need help, and the faster you learn how to ask for it, will relieve more pressure from your plate.

Once I get that hug with a reminder, I start to set a course for the week. I do not fill up that week with more errands or work that I can't handle. I lighten the load. I write post-it notes around the house that say "breathe," so I sit down and take a breath each day. I'll draw a bubble bath or pick a funny movie to watch. It's a "cut yourself some slack" kinda week so you can grieve but still be present in your life.

When the day comes, you may feel blessed to have had that time, or you may feel emotionally drained and sad. I'm at a 50/50 split of feeling blessed and sad. When I have many times of the latter, I fall into that day. No work, no chores, just self-care, mostly watching movies all day on the couch. Whatever you deem as your perfect self-care is your choice, but once again, these times will always come around, and you have to learn to live through it.

Healing Tools for Transformation

This section is to provide innovative methods to aid in your healing journey. I do not have all the answers, and I am not a doctor, so I use my personal experiences to help others through their turmoil. There are many medical books on grief that I implore you to pick up and read for your own knowledge, but this book is meant to tell a story and use my lessons for the betterment of others.

"To live life is to suffer, to survive is to find some meaning in the suffering" - **Nietzsche**

This is one of my favorite quotes my brother sent to me during my first year of complicated grief. Life is about suffering; without it, we couldn't understand and experience happiness to the fullest capacity. Time and dedication need to be at play to understand suffering and uncover the truth behind it so you may survive freely without emotional restraints.

Understanding the Many Shades of Grief. I urge you to read further into the different types of grief, but I want to provide you with a broad overview that may shed light on the expectations of your journey. I had no idea there were so many different grief associations, but once you digest them, you can better grasp your stages and learn how to help your mind feel calm.

Anticipatory Grief: This often starts when a person gets a significant diagnosis, and their health begins to deteriorate. You begin to imagine what life could have or would have been. There are many emotions that you may feel cannot be discussed because that person is still living. Guilt for this grief may also come into play.

Normal Grief: There are no guidelines to what normal grief looks like. In fact, I almost didn't write about it because it's so obscure. Most relate it to any response that resembles what you may expect grief to resemble. For example, some sources say it's the ability to feel acceptance for the loss. But really, what is normal?

Complicated Grief: This is sometimes called persistent complex bereavement disorder, where the feelings of loss are debilitating and don't improve even after time passes. These painful emotions are so long-lasting and severe that one cannot recover from the loss and resume their lives. Often complicated grief stems from sudden, tragic, or violent loss, to name a few.

Delayed Grief: This is the postponement of reaction or emotion to the loss until a later date. The initiation of this type could be from another life experience, maybe a divorce as an example, or even something unrelated.

Cumulative Grief: When many losses occur within a short window of time, leaving little room for recovery from the initial loss in order to process the next**Chronic/Prolonged Grief:** A form of grief that lasts for an extended period of time, with feelings of hopelessness and disbelief that the loss is real or even avoidance of anything related to the loss.

Masked Grief: A type of grief reaction when the person experiences symptoms and behavior which causes them difficulty, but they do not see or recognize the fact that they are related to the loss.

Shadow Grief: Defined as "a dull ache in the background of one's feelings that remains fairly constant and that, under certain circumstances and on certain occasions, comes bubbling to the surface, sometimes in the form of tears, sometimes not, but always in the form of sadness and a mild sense of anxiety." 1 This type typically comes once you have traveled further into your journey and can span a lifetime. It is natural and genuine. The ways I lived through this were by the examples listed above when preparing for a special "once was" occasion.

Abbreviated Grief: This type is exactly what it sounds like, grief that seemed to be dealt with quickly but genuinely. Typically, this grief occurs when something or someone has replaced the recently deceased with a new love or friendship. It also may happen because someone has started the process of Anticipatory Grief for someone diagnosed with an illness. So by the time the person passes, the bereaved have already begun the journey of healing. Another factor for this grief is someone not feeling safe due to emotional strife. Some are scared to "let go" of themselves and open up to pain because it can be frightening. In times like these, it's best to set goals of healing such as "I will allow myself 15 minutes of sadness and then get back to work," as that allotment of emotion feels safe.

Distorted Grief: This unfortunate type of grief can present with self-destructive behaviors, extreme feelings of anger or guilt, and hostility.

Inhibited Grief: When someone consciously wishes to keep their grief private and show no outward sign of the grief process. Sometimes physical manifestation can occur when someone suppresses their healing process.

Secondary Loss in Grief: After the primary loss has happened, it sets into motion secondary losses. This may create a sense that one is losing everything. Examples of secondary loss include loss of a support system, loss of dreams, loss of financial security, and loss of a chosen lifestyle.

Absent Grief: Typically, the result of denial and a complete facade, the person does not show any signs related to grief or acknowledge the loss.

Collective Grief: This is experienced by a group of people within a community, city, or nation stemmed from a natural disaster, death of a public figure, or terrorist attack.

Disenfranchised Grief: Dr. Kenneth Doka (Professor Emeritus at the Graduate School of The College of New Rochelle and Senior Consultant to the Hospice Foundation of America) coined this term, "Grief that persons experience when they incur a loss that is not or cannot be openly acknowledged, socially sanctioned or publicly mourned." Death of a pet, infertility, death by a drug overdose, loss of a home, divorce, death of an ex-spouse or ex-partner all fall under this category. You may feel, or someone has made you feel like you don't have the right to grieve. There are five categories into which these types of grief may fall.

- **The loss isn't seen as worthy of grief**

- **The relationship is stigmatized**
- **The mechanism of death is stigmatized**
- **The person grieving is not recognized as a griever**
- **The way someone is grieving is stigmatized**

Mourning is Not Regulated. Well-meaning friends and family will try to set a time-period for your grief. A time when they think you should be back to normal or "over it." They do this to try and help you feel like you can move on apart from grief and be happy. Not only is this one of the unhealthiest concepts to accept, but it will also cause more internal turmoil in the future. It is your right to grieve for however long you choose. It is your right to feel any socially deemed uncomfortable emotion and verbalize that for as long as you choose. You make the decisions for yourself. No timetable or person can take away your right to heal correctly, unless you let them.

One of my favorite activists and authors is Marianne Williamson. She takes inspiration to an elite level. She states, "The avoidance of sadness decreases our capacity to learn from it...In avoiding our sadness, we avoid our lives." [2]

Avoidance can become a comfortable attribute to some, but by succumbing to self-neglect, you deny your mind the understanding of pain. As she states, you end up avoiding your life if you choose this path. Pain is a part of life and growth, and although we don't like to experience it, without it, we are a one-dimensional, single facetted being. When you understand the root of the pain and expand beyond it then you have conquered. You have survived a time that changed you because you didn't allow your mourning to be regulated. You invested in the misunderstood pain, made it comprehendible and applicable to a better future.

Find Joy in the Unexpected. Finding joy during the grief process can be difficult, but I encourage you to be open to joy in whatever capacity it presents itself. Although, the unexpected moments felt like small wins that would make my whole day, I found and accepted that joy.

I was genuinely surprised when I was sent four books called the Continuing Care Series from the bereavement support group of the funeral home that cared for Nick. These books would come at different stages of my grief process, and they were honestly some of the most helpful books. They were only 23 pages each but chalked full of heartfelt and knowledgeable information. Your funeral home may have them or similar books on site for you, but if not, this is a purchase that is worth every dollar. Along with the books came letters that not only provided care for my soul but gave personal perspective. I was taught great lessons from these letters, and they made me feel like I was not forgotten.

I was also sent a book of prayers from Nick's college called the Potpourri of Prayers, written by Siena College. It felt so lovely to receive these gifts from places I did not expect. When I opened this book, I didn't turn to page one. Instead I opened up to a prayer in the middle called, "Remembered Joy." I knew this was a sign from Nick, which made me cry and feel comfort simultaneously.

Remembered Joy

The Beauty Within Tragedy

Don't grieve for me, for now I'm free!

I followed the plan God laid for me.

I saw His face, I heard His call,

I took His hand and left it all...

I could not stay another day.

To love, to laugh, to work or play;

Tasks left undone must stay that way.

And if my parting has left a void,

Then fill it with remembered joy.

A friendship shared, a laugh, a kiss...

Ah yes, these things I, too, shall miss.

My life's been full, I've savored much:

Good times, good friends, a loved one's touch.

Perhaps my time seemed all too brief –

Don't shorten yours with undue grief.

Be not burdened with tears of sorrow,

Enjoy the sunshine of the morrow.

At times my story would be shared with strangers and was immediately followed by a huge hug from the listener. These hugs were unexpected moments of joy that brought me more comfort than I would have imagined. A hug from a stranger hits the heart better than you would think when battling a dark time.

Seek Help. A trained psychologist or psychiatrist can provide a perspective that may not have been present in your mind. There are many who specialize in grief who can to help and give advice to move forward. I went to the same therapist that helped Nick and me during our marital struggles simply because she knew my entire back story, and she always opened my mind to new ways of understanding pain. If you don't know where to start in your journey, this is a great first step. We are a population that excels by asking for help when we do not have the foundational tools to take the next step. So, ask and try to seek out help. If you have never gone to a professional or have preconceived negative thoughts, that's ok. But when all your emotions are new and unknown, it's the perfect time to try something new with a person trained to help you in the best way possible. All you have to do is trust in the process.

You may also be as daring as I was to try an energy healer. I got to a place where I would try any and everything to make myself feel better. So when I learned of energy healers, I was intrigued. The study behind energy medicine is that individuals can channel healing energy into a patient yielding positive results. The scientific explanation is that all things emit an energy field, and energy medicine, based on quantum physics, uses this field in healing practices. There have been references stating this practice goes back over 3000 years. It includes all the modalities that focus on the body's energy communication and all energy concepts: light, sound, electro-magnetism, body, mind, and spirit. Practitioners state that energy can stagnate in the body where there has been physical injury or emotional pain. By seeking treatment, the healer aims to help the flow of energy and remove blocks. I completed a handful of sessions and was in awe of how the treatment made me feel lighter, freer, and calm. If this is out of your comfort zone, think about when you are around a group of upbeat and positive people on a day you are feeling down. Their energy almost immediately is shared with you, lifting you up from your somber state and you become heightened to a state of happiness. This is the perfect time to try something new, you are in the perfect place to explore and grow.

Acupuncture is another avenue, like energy healing. It will pinpoint the body's area of physical or emotional pain to flush out the toxins in your organs harboring the impurities. It has been a practice of Chinese medicine for over 3000 years and can be a great treatment for depression. This is one form of aid that can replace medication if you do not wish to be prescribed anything. Acupuncture is based on specific anatomic points called "acupoints" stimulated using tiny, thin needles that correct the flow of energy, known as qi or chi, thus restoring balance and relieving pain. This treatment can be used for many disorders such as digestive disorders, hormone imbalances, and chronic disease. As mentioned earlier in the book, I sought out acupuncture when trying to conceive a baby, and although I did not revisit this treatment post-trauma, I most definitely should have done so. If for nothing else, the 20-25 minutes of treatment let my body and mind reach a state of Zen, and I walked out feeling rejuvenated. That statement is not to underplay the importance of this practice but to give you a glimpse into another outlet of healing in its simplest form.

I am blessed to have an Uncle that is the Senior Pastor of our church. He has always been a fantastic messenger and storyteller, paralleling the Bible to everyday life. I called upon him many times to express my inner turmoil, and it was always met with great wisdom and calming solace. He always had the right words to help guide me down the path God knew I was destined to take. If you are a person of faith that attends worship, lean on a messenger of God for spiritual guidance. If you do not attend a worship place but seek guidance, turn to "couch church," as a friend of mine calls it. From the comfort of your couch, you can watch services of many affiliations online or from your TV to gain spiritual enlightenment.

Start a Journey Journal. A powerful tool of expression is writing. It can remain private or be used as an outlet of expression to those you choose to hear your thoughts. Find a journal you want to jot your thoughts down in or create a journal on your computer and start writing how you feel every day. In six months, you can look back and see how far you've come or pinpoint places you think you should revisit for further healing. In a year, you may be able to smile with pride at how far the journey has taken you to this point.

This journal is your reflection of emotion that will mold you into a different version of yourself, the best version. You can write goals, poems, songs, compelling quotes, resonate with your state of emotion, or write mantras to help you get through a week. Some of the greatest compositions stem from the darkest of times because those are the most vulnerable, raw human emotions that we may not speak of but can all relate to on some level.

My journal ended up becoming a blog and thus birthing a company called L4 – Livin' Life, Lovin' Life. I wanted to help people find positivity through the pain again, so I would write articles and use music to help others find a sense of peace as they traveled their course.

Make a Lesson List. After the first year of grief, I wrote down a list of all the lessons I learned. Maybe your list is one of goals to achieve, new hobbies to discover, or memories of your deceased loved one you never want to forget. Whatever it's comprised of, lists help keep our mind focused and can be used as reference tools when we have a down day. At the end of this book I'm sharing my list of lessons as it pertains to my grief journey and possibly they will resonate with you.

Write a Letter. This was something I learned from my amazing therapist. Write a letter to the one you lost. Maybe you are mad at them for leaving, desperate to touch them again, craving to hear their voice, write that and more in your letter. All the things you wished you said or want to say again, all the plans you had that you now must surrender, and maybe what you have endured in their absence. This task is a way to place your loved one close, memorialize your life with them and state the pain you feel since they have moved on. It also makes your current situation real and psychologically allows your mind to accept the loss.

I used this assignment when I had my miscarriages. I wrote about all the plans we had for them as they grew and the love we had for them while they were in my womb. It was an awful letter to write, but one that gave them a voice through my words. It allowed my dreams to be valid and not just memories I may forget. That letter gave me a slight sense of peace, it wasn't the fix to any prolonged pain, but it did become one of the many tools that got me to a better place. Below is my letter.

~ Letter to My Angel Babies ~

Dear Sienna, Gabriella, Tennison, Ainsley, Brayden, Gavin, and Callen,

Our precious babies of hope, light, joy, love, and wonderment! You will all forever be in my heart and imprinted on my soul until the day I meet you in Heaven. Your Daddy and I cherished every moment I felt you grow inside me and carry that sentiment as you live on with him. The joys you gave to us were times of purity and sanctimonious bliss that can't be relayed in words, but I know you feel.

As crazy as this sounds, I feel I knew each one of you without ever seeing your faces, and I think about what it would have been like growing up with you.

We had such amazing plans for an adventurous and happy life. Being your Mommy for even a short time gave me the unrelenting courage to fight off anything that might have stood in your way as you grew. No children would have been so loved and adored as you. Nothing is taken for granted, and no long tiresome days would be taken for granted. The bad times would still be good times, and the good times would be more than great.

I'm so mad you were taken from us and desperately want to see who you all would have become. I hate more than anything that you weren't given a chance at life. My saving grace in all this is knowing you are with your Daddy, and he gets to love you and spoil you and do all the things we talked about together. I don't speak to you enough, and that's probably because my pain still runs too deep for even my understanding, but I hope to be better. I'm sorry I didn't grieve each of you as I should have at the time; I feel I have disrespected your memory partially because I didn't do my part to heal properly and mourn you significantly.

Every day you all are in my heart, and I know we would have given you all the love we had and more, showing you off to anyone that would look or listen— spoiling you too much and laughing through the days as a family. I miss each of you, my precious angels, and love you more than anything!

Love,

Mommy

<u>Read Books.</u> Maybe you aren't a book reader per se, but there are so many things we never knew we didn't know until we read about them. My interest in reading books calmed me down and provided enlightenment. What helped balance out my life again were books that gave insight and understanding to what I was living through. Books that gave a perspective I didn't think of before. These weren't all 300 page books with extreme messages, some were short versions of helpful stories, others were full of different prayers and some inspired poems.

The books mentioned in the paragraphs above sent to me by the funeral home were four of the simplest reads, but with the most impact. The author, Doug Manning, describes the layers of grief during the stages of your first year.

"Grief is not like a disease that can be cured. Grief is an amputation of a part of you that must be healed over, but will never be replaced."
3

The Pain of Grief – **Book One**

The Reality of Grief – **Book Two**

The Dimensions of Grief – **Book Three**

The Journey of Grief – **Book Four**

The New York Times deems the next book as "One of the ten most recommended books by clinical psychologists to their clients." It's another simple, yet impactful book, based in psychological practice, poetry and problem solving. The entire book is in bullet point format in order to hit home the most important parts. "You are much more than the emotional wound you are currently suffering. Don't lose sight of that."

How To Survive The Loss of a Love, by Harold H. Bloomfield, M.D. |Melba Colgrove, PH.D. | Peter McWilliams

I was given a very special book, by a dear family member that I keep in my nightstand to this day as a reference to how God responds to our lives. This book is a devotional read filled with heartfelt stories, experiences and adorable illustrations.

"You may be in a cave, but you have a choice: You can sit in the dark, or you can diamond-mine your difficulties."

Under God's Umbrella, by Holly Gerth

All of the books mentioned above are inspiring, helpful and full of impressive knowledge. They all carry a lightness to them which is why I'm recommending them in my book. Sometimes we need to let our minds relax as we digest important information for healing. Other times we need to dive deeper in order to uncover enlightenment.

One of my dear sorority sisters, Kate, turned me on to Marianne Williamson. You read earlier how she is one of my favorite activists, but her book transformed my way of thinking about myself, my grief and my entire lifetime journey.

"The ego keeps us bound to the illusion that we exist entirely subject to the material world, when in fact the world is nothing but the projection of our thoughts."

Tears To Triumph, by: Marianne Williamson

Whether you choose self-help, or self-discovery books as I like to call them, or ones that take you to a far-away land, it doesn't matter. What matters is you're expanding and imagining, letting your mind breathe through other's words, inadvertently tattooing healing tools onto your heart

Write Down Quotes. In addition to your list, writing down quotes and keeping them on hand can be extremely helpful during times of despair. You may have some quotes you've always turned to that now have a different meaning and application for your life. I remember times when I would search online for inspiration looking up such words as motivation, grief, love, healing, time, and loss among others. Whatever I was feeling, I would search, and low and behold, there was always a quote or line I could draw upon.

Once I found one that hit my heart, I would write it down in my quote journal. It was a smaller version of my journey journal that I carried with me every time I left the house. The imprint on the cover read, "On To The Next Adventure," which I thought was a great mantra for myself. My dear Mom bought me this little journal that carries some of the best quotes and motivational thoughts I could compile for myself. Thanks, Mom!

You never know when a moment of pain will hit harder than usual, or a trigger will occur, so in those times I turn to those quotes to help rebalance my mind.

<u>Be Entrenched in Nature.</u> If you want to look up all the scientific studies relating to how nature immeasurably affects our well-being, please be my guests. There are many.

For the sake of sparing you percentage ratios of brain functionality with natural elements versus without, all that needs mentioning is that being outside will positively shift your emotional state. Shifting your environment to a natural setting can improve your mental health just by being in it. Studies show how people who live by and view large bodies of water regularly live a more tranquil life. There is a calm simplicity when you're outside.

You feel the sun penetrating B12 and Vitamin D into your skin, a breeze that carries a hint of peace, and birds that sing a soothing melody. Bring that book you chose to read outside. Take a walk, and while on this walk, look a little closer at the beauty of the flowers, the purity of the snow or the gracefulness of the rolling waves. These are things you probably took for granted before your trauma, but now you can be happy just witnessing their presence and the feeling you get by living in them.

Forest Bathing has become a popular practice although the theory behind it has been around for a very long time. This ecotherapy now has guided tours through some of the worlds most beautiful forests. The premise is simple, recognizing that the natural world is imperative to human health. You don't need to find a forrest or a tour, walking in the grass and grounding yourself while being immersed in the physical feel, the harmonious sounds and the sweet smells in a place you find beauty is perfect.

Do for Others | _Be with Others._ "It is in the shelter of each other that people live," Irish Proverb. We have spoken about how self-reflection and care are of the utmost importance when dealing with grief. But there is something to be said about doing a nice gesture for someone else, even when you feel like the world is ending. For example, drop a bouquet of flowers to a friend that has helped you survive or run an errand for someone who is too sick to get out of bed. By doing these acts of kindness, we remember that we are capable of living with grief, and can still feel happiness by doing for others while enduring our own pain.

If I didn't have my tribe of the most unbelievable people, my first year of healing would have been so much worse. Your closest and truest will be there for you always, never setting a time limit on how you "should be" feeling. At month seven and eight of the first year, when others think you should be moving on, these are the people that will still ask what they can do to help. In years two, three, and four they will also make sure you are feeling supported and loved, by remembering anniversaries, sending a text of a fond memory shared by all or simply checking on you. Cling to the group that guards your heart and protects you from things you cannot. Sit in a room with them and watch a movie if you don't want to talk, but be with others. Seclusion can be healthy as you work through grief milestones, but too much isolation will dim your light.

In being with others, remember to choose the right people to let into your vulnerable space. Toxic individuals or those that may exercise destructive behavior will not benefit your life ever, but especially now. I had a group of well-meaning individuals that came back into my life during my first grief year and I got sucked into their "party" ways too much. The pain was masked and numbed as I lived in an alternative reality, and it was a healing setback. There are times when you simply don't care during this process, that's also okay. But what's not okay is never rising to the surface again to take a much needed breath and a restart.

Don't Ignore the Signs. There will be signs, and you may miss a lot of them in the beginning. Some will argue that these signs are figments of a psychological manifestation created to soften our pain. Whatever you believe is your belief. But one day you will have a dream that carries a message from your loved one, or a spirit animal that always comes around when needed most, or a song played that was shared on days of special occasions, or perhaps a perfume/cologne will waft your way when speaking about them.

Some long for these signs and get discouraged or angered when they don't appear right away. It would help if you were patient, overcome the initial shock and give your mind time to open back up again. I remember all my friends were having dreams of Nick, and I didn't have one. I was so mad and felt pissed that his own wife couldn't get this gift. Then, almost six months later, I had a dream where Nick talked so clearly to me, and even though the dream was not all rainbows, I still felt him and his love.

Nick was a tremendous athlete, and his favorite sport was hockey. He played his whole life, and as he got older, he played in a men's league, which is where I learned the game. Nick wore a yellow helmet from his college days that remained his signature. When he passed, we planted a tree in his honor that bloomed yellow flowers. One day when I was taking a run, I started crying uncontrollably and sat down in the grass.

As I sat, I felt a flicker brush my arm, and when I lifted my head, I saw a yellow butterfly fluttering in front of my face. It didn't fly away, yet it stayed in my line of sight as if it had something to say. I knew it was Nick letting me know he was fine, and I would be too. So I got up to run home, and that yellow butterfly flew next to me the entire way. After that, a yellow butterfly would accompany me on parts of my runs for months to come. I still receive visits from these gorgeous creatures, and I know it's Nick letting me know he is always around.

Travel. After I resigned from my job, I packed up my car and drove to one of my favorite places on earth, Nashville. I had the luxury of staying there for a month, where I started learning guitar, wrote music, recorded a song, and explored the surrounding towns. While going away for a month is not feasible for all, changing your surroundings is a great way to gain perspective of yourself. I spent most of that time being by myself and learned how to be fine with being alone. Being alone and comfortable in that space does not mean you are lonely. It means that you can survive without leaning on the person you thought you would have with you forever. Maybe choose a place you have never been before but longed to see or take a weekend trip away from your daily life. This is not intended to be an escape from your problems, but it's meant to create new opportunities and experiences for yourself within your new life. Or, if anything, you may just breathe a little easier for a few days. Finding self-preservation is key to enduring the long ride.

Meditate. There is an art to meditation. You can look up different forms and practices and tailor them to what suits your needs. The reason for this tool is to set aside time to only be with yourself. When you meditate, the vibrational tone resonates throughout your body to consume yourself with harmonious energy. If you're uncomfortable with audible meditation, setting aside 10 minutes to close your eyes and listen to background music will help slow your breathing, reduce anxiety and release pain.

Get Creative. Your journey may heighten your creativity. Maybe you feel the urge to draw, paint or sing a song, do it! Perhaps you never knew you were an expert cake decorator, or you could write poetry. Find a new hobby you always wanted to pick up. Releasing energy into something creative allows our mind to feel useful and gives us a sense of pride that we accomplished creating something.

Listen to Music. If you haven't picked up on a subtle passion of mine, it's music. I sing, write songs, and I use to play the piano (I get to pick that up again). Music was the best outlet for me. It was calming when I needed ease. It was rejuvenating when I needed motivation. It was happiness when I needed uplifting, and it was somber when I needed understanding of darkness. You've heard the phrase that music is a universal language, and this couldn't be truer during your time of struggle. There is a song for every emotion and a feeling you will draw from that song that will alter your mind. Try new genres you may think you don't enjoy. Listen to the melody and the storyline, and you will be surprised at how many songs resonate with your situation.

Head Above Water – **Avril Lavigne**

This song came out when I needed to hear it most. Avril wrote this song regarding her tumultuous battle with Lime Disease, but it manifested differently to me and gave me the strength I needed to get up. That's the beauty of music. Each person can hear the same song and relate it to their own lives in the way they need for comfort. This song embodies the mental struggle we go through to fight for ourselves. She sings about how her life is worth fighting for and how her struggle won't pull her overboard, it truly touched me when I heard it the first time and now every time thereafter. I wrote the below on my L4 Blog mixing my love of music and writing:

"Fighting for yourself is so hard! We fight for others, beliefs, opinions, and beyond. But when we need to pull the sword out and slay the demons ahead for our own well-being, we find it to be heavy. It is! Lifting your own sword will be the hardest thing you have to do because it's only YOU that can do it. Your support system will help you hold that sword, but you are the reason your life will change. Always fight to choose the path that loves you the most. Allow your voice to be your driving force and make it count.

Putting Acceptance and Tools into Action. The first grief year is when you should actively schedule time. Make the time to heal and choose how you want to chart your course. The only way you can dig yourself out of the grave you feel you're in is by taking the first step. Find the desire to dig. If there's no desire to help yourself over time, then part of your process should be charting a course towards medical support. Next, seek out the professional aid that will help you pick up that shovel of motivation. You are vulnerable and need to accept the things that have changed so you can pick up the tools of healing. Don't be a superhero but be super in your pursuit to live fully after tragedy.

"One does not become enlightened by imagining figures of light, but by making the darkness conscious." – **Carl Jung**

Brotherly Love

He's home! After three years my brother, Ryan, moved back home to Florida. Our whole family was so excited to get him back, but we had no idea it would be short-lived.

Ryan was always by my side, my best friend and confidant. When we fought, it was fleeting, and I'm proud to say we only encountered a few blowups. We led utterly different lives, but we always found commonality and shared interests. I have great memories of making him perform Disney songs with me, always reluctant, but he did it. We would play video games, remember Tetris and Zelda? They were my two favorites. Also, going to the movies was one of our favorite things to do as a family, and we saw many.

His mind was one of genius status and he tested as such. School was so easy for him that it blew my mind. He flew through physics as if he was saying his ABCs. His passion for life and understanding of all things technical were impressive. He learned everything there was to know about cars, from rebuilding a chassis to the 0-60 run of any make and model. He had an affinity for guns and engrossed himself in learning about every model and their specifications, how to handle a firearm properly, shooting, and the strategy and science behind it.

He loved every angle of this field, so much so that he became a certified NRA Instructor and expert in guns and ammunition. He learned to code and would develop websites. He was just as versed and comfortable with the technical as he was with the creative. He would build beautiful digital graphics and had an eye for design work. We spent hours listening and dissecting music together. He was a true teacher and had a knack for explaining even the most difficult of concepts to all who were interested. He could explain the String Theory just as easily as he could tell you the plot from a movie and the hidden symbolism behind it. He was one of my greatest teachers and expanded my mind to things I wouldn't have normally found interesting.

As the older sister, I thought I was the one protecting him when in reality he was always looking out for me. When we all had only land lines, he picked up phone calls to see what boys were calling when he was 8-years-old and I was twelve. Always the protective brother throughout our whole lives. At a very young age, we would travel to Sun Valley, Idaho for the summers with another family, who happened to be our best friends. Since we lived in Florida, going out west was a real treat, and we had the best of both worlds. From beaches to mountains, flamingos to horses, we experienced two different ways of living. There was a peacefulness about our time in Sun Valley. The air seemed a little cleaner, the people a bit nicer, and we had many adventures that we didn't get to experience in Florida. For 13 summers, this was our second home and as often as possible, it is still a place my family loves to travel.

As the years went on, our bond was still the same, but we started to shift the paths of our lives. I was the teenager that followed the rules, and Ryan would always bend or completely break them. When we speak of him, a statement pops up. "he lived a spirited life." On one hand, that's a very poignant statement, his life was spirited in all aspects and, for the most part, that carried positive attributes. But this is also a nice way of saying he went down the rabbit hole of addiction.

As passionate as he was, he also battled with a level of anxiety that took years to diagnose. Social anxiety kept him from participating in a slew of experiences that he might have loved if equipped with tools to combat that disorder sooner. He was always in his head about life and the meaning behind why things do or do not happen—dissecting every detail until it would drive him mad, almost as if he could never have calm thoughts.

I believe that this is the reason he chose drugs and alcohol. They were an escape from the rampant thoughts that flushed his mind every minute of the day. Growing up, he always spoke a mile a minute, and for long spurts of time, no one else could get a word in. But if he spoke like this, I can't imagine what was going on in his mind that wasn't being discussed. His self-medication was a release from the thoughts and inner turmoil he lived with daily.

Therapists and psychiatrists said he had bipolar depression and he was medicated improperly for years. He knew this wasn't the correct diagnosis, but his voice was dismissed because he wasn't a professional. This is a constant reminder to me about always advocating for your health. Ryan knew this was wrong, so he kept trying to find answers to understand his own mind. He read many books learning how to use his thoughts as power, looking up scientific articles explaining brain synapses while understanding the "contextual" roadmap of how the mind operates. Eventually, the doctors listened and diagnosed him with severe anxiety, and he was placed on the proper medication. However, it resulted in panic attacks, confusion, anger and rage. He was a strong man with a soft heart, but he was a different person when red would glass over his mind.

Years of watching him struggle with life were challenging for our family. A constant state of worry filled each of our lives. Until he walked through that door for the night, I was never settled. I was always wondering if the next phone call was the one describing his end. When I went away to college, I tasked Showboat with watching over him. They were very close, and Ryan looked up to him tremendously. They shared the same intellectual capacity and interests; they had a special bond. Showboat would keep me updated when Ryan would call on him during tough times. I would call Showboat when I found out trouble was looming, and he would drop everything to be there for Ryan. The worry never stopped and grew as the years went by.

He tried rehab, a fleeting success, and an experience he felt was a joke. Most likely because he didn't want to let go of the only way he knew how to get relief from the games his mind would play. I remember a time I asked him to describe what he feels every day. His answer was "complete mental chaos." In an effort to cope differently, Ryan began studying meditation. This helped him tremendously. Controlled breathing in a space where he felt serenity was his magic potion. Yet, it wasn't enough to jump out of the rabbit hole.

One day it was time for a location change. He packed his bags and moved to Sun Valley, hoping this environment would allow him to breathe a bit lighter and enjoy the things that brought him such joy. It's a simpler life out there, and we all thought it was the best idea given all the challenges and heartache he endured in Florida. Idaho provided different opportunities for him to find peace in nature. He enjoyed snowboarding, off-roading, and riding through the deep snows in the cold winter months, outdoor range practice, meditation by the rivers, and walks through the woods in the warmer months. He wanted to start a new life and try once again to climb out of that hole.

He began a new program in AA and seemed to be in a place of first step recovery. While there, he met a girl and fell in love. We all had such hope for a beautiful future for them both. Cut from similar cloth, they understood each other and the paths they lived through. All seemed to be heading in the right direction, and then we were given the news that they were expecting a baby. This news brought shock to all of us, but I remember thinking that this gift is going to be the one that changes Ryan. The only thing that can shake a man like him is falling in love with a child of his own as he learns what love means. I was also scared for him as well. What if even the love of a child wasn't enough to help salvage his life? Could he be the parent I knew he wanted to be, or would the rabbit hole suck him back down when things became overwhelming? Even though I had many fears, I knew he would try his best to be the best. I knew our family would be there for him and his child, and if he did fall, we would pick him back up. So, I pushed the negative out and let my faith in a positive future remain the steady thought.

The news of new life came two months after Nick died, carrying great joy for our family's future. When Ryan called me, I heard the hesitation in his voice. He prefaced our conversation by saying he wants to tell me something, but he almost felt bad sharing his joy. Once he finally told me he was having a baby, I screamed with joy for them. I told him not to feel an ounce of guilt regarding our different situations. I didn't want him to stifle his happiness because of my heartache. That's not fair to him. The reality was I did feel immense joy and happiness for him and hope for our lives. I was touched that he took my feelings into great consideration. I found out later he even talked to my Mom about how badly he felt. He was genuinely selfless like that, wanting to make sure my feelings were validated if I did have sadness creep in.

About a half hour after we got off the phone, I thought about how life can really be unfair. After all the years of trying to have a baby, the financial commitment and the grief that filled our lives, the gift Nick and I desperately wanted came so easily to my brother. It was a deep breath moment for me, but not one of jealousy, more of acceptance. This is life and no matter what happens this is what's supposed to happen, even if I didn't understand the why. The reality was, though, I did know the why. I wasn't supposed to be a widow left to raise our children without their father. My path didn't include a life of connection with Nick's family. So I was spared the horrible explanation to my children that their father had died and the tragic way he did.

I was spared the sorrow I would have for my kids grieving their Dad for a lifetime. I was spared the nightmares of the plane crash and their Dad in a fiery blaze. My unborn children were spared a life of living without their Dad. This may seem like an incredibly selfish way to accept my reality, but it's what helped pull me out of my rabbit hole. There is not one day I don't wish I had any of my seven children we lost with me, and we would live through that nightmare together, but I understand why now they are with Nick and not with me. Nick gets to have all seven, surrounding him in surreal, Heavenly joy. No complications, no fear, just peace and my heart is full thinking of that notion. I eventually expressed those thoughts in full to Ryan, and I could hear a sense of relief in his voice, which made me happy.

Months passed, and the anticipation for little miss Isabella's arrival was growing. Along with that anticipation came realizations we hoped would never be reality. The woman we thought we knew and whom Ryan committed to was not the person we thought. Her pregnancy brought back all those feelings of worry we use to have with Ryan. AA was a mask that gave an alibi to someone trying to live a life of lies. Maybe her addiction never was turned into recovery, and we were all fooled. Her past became a shining beacon of her future, and the unborn baby was paying the price. I'm not exactly sure at what point Ryan decided to turn back to alcohol, but he did, which didn't help the situation they were living through as a couple. Luckily my brother never went back to the depths of his addiction as in years prior, but the self-medication was back in play. His stress level went through the roof as he pleaded with her to quit anything during the pregnancy. So we uttered many prayers for a healthy baby, and thus began the destruction of a dream I had for my brother's future.

Finally, the time came when Isabella was ready to join the world. My parents were already in Idaho preparing for the day they would meet their first grandchild. Then Isabella Marie was born on July 22, 2016, at 10:36 pm. We were all blessed with a beautiful baby girl and all seemed right in the world. I flew out two weeks later to meet my niece. Mind you, flying had become very difficult for me at this point. I knew all the reasons why flying is safe, but the images of Nick's horrific crash still ran run through my mind and made it difficult to step onto that plane.

It's still amazing to me that no matter how hard I worked to only think of positive thoughts, the darkest and most grotesque pictures popped into my head as I boarded three flights to meet the miracle in our family. Xanax became my friend because I needed to be medicated to fly, and still do sometimes. So naturally as one tries not to think of the bad that could happen, a slightly bad situation happened on my last and shortest flight to Idaho. About 20 minutes into the journey, the captain gets on the speaker and says they need to turn the plane around and land back at Salt Lake City airport. I'm thinking engine trouble, fuel leak, navigation system shutdown, but as I'm closing my eyes and trying to think of rainbows and butterflies, all I see is Nick's plane engorged in a fiery blaze.

These are the moments that make life hard to live through. I know deep down, if there was a true emergency, more fuss would be made, more announcements regarding safety would be heard, but my heart still raced as the captain turned the plane around. We landed back safely in Salt Lake, and I waited an hour to re-board the plane and head out on our journey one last time. We landed safely for the second time, and with my legs shaking, I bolted off the plane and fell into my Mom and Dad's arms. Relief set in, and I blocked out any thoughts of my return trip home.

The Beauty Within Tragedy

I began breathing lighter with excitement built up to see this precious baby. Luckily Ryan lived a mile from the airport, so my anticipation only needed to last a few more minutes. We pulled up to his townhome, and Ryan was just getting home as well. As he took out the car seat and I walked up to see his daughter for the first time, complete love and warmth came over my body. She was perfect, and the look of pride on my brother's face is forever etched in my mind. He looked like a new man to me, and he was, he was a Dad. It was such a surreal moment to see him in this new role, but I felt a sense of peace for him, which I could see in his eyes as well. This type of happiness can't be described, only felt, and I saw that he felt true happiness as a Father. This is what I wanted for Ryan's life, a purpose he felt in the physical sense and the emotional. Someone now relied on him entirely and completely to be present, aware, and provide the most love he could give. He got to make his daughter feel safe and secure. He was always trying to find meaning and never fully captured a true sense of his place in the world until now, until he discovered genuine selfless love.

We walked inside, sat down, and Isabella was placed in my arms. I was immediately overtaken with piercing pings of love for this child. Her birth was the salvation of our family, the joy we needed to jumpstart our lives again. As Isabella entered our lives, an amount of pain exited. I'm still not able to gauge what amount, but I know that life became a little lighter and a heck of a lot fuller. Her being was one of hope and grace for our lives. Her smile broke through the darkest days, and her infectious coos softened blows. She will probably never know what a gift her birth was, but I will be sure to let her know as often as I can for the rest of my life.

The Beauty Within Tragedy

Before Isabella's birth, I wasn't sure how I would fully internalize her arrival. I knew beyond any doubt that I would fall in love with her, be overjoyed for Ryan, and feel sheer happiness. But would I regress back to a state of loss for my own children, knowing I was on the course to give our family the first grandchild? Would I feel any sense of jealousy or sadness? Would I fall victim to the grief I never fully dealt with when I lost each one of my children? I had no answers to these questions and had no way of preparing to deal with any one of these emotions, so I thought I would just have to live through whatever came.

I didn't honestly feel any of these things before her birth but knew I might have to prepare to battle myself and find peace with that now. What I did know was the past eight months gave me enough pain so I wasn't going to waste time thinking too much about what I might feel in a moment I couldn't possibly understand. I didn't spiral down a dark hole or feel sorry for myself. I didn't second guess my love for this beauty or fall victim to anything concerning my own path. I only felt joy in all the different senses and levels that word carries. I feel this is a testament to the relationship Ryan and I shared; we were never boastful, jealous of each other's accomplishments, spiteful, or manipulative.

We were always accepting of each other and our differences, we were understanding of our differing viewpoints, and even embraced them. We celebrated goals and cheered on life together. Naturally, we had negative moments, but the foundation of our bond was truly unbreakable, and when joy happened to one, the other shared in that feeling without restraint. So why I thought for one second that any negative emotions would be present was silly, but on the other hand, those emotions are very raw and authentic and could very well have been felt. I'm sure these natural emotions are had by many people dealing with similar situations, and there is no shame in it. I was grateful that I had one less thing to work on for myself, and I could enjoy our blessed gift fully and completely.

The next two weeks were full of cuddles, naptime on the couch with Isabella laying peacefully in my arms, laughter that seemed louder, and new shared brother/sister moments of raising a child that were priceless. I also took this time to try and get to know Ryan's girlfriend better. I had high hopes for their future, praying this birth would change perspectives and provide the desire to recover from past self-abuse. I hoped this would be a fresh start, and they could live happily ever after understanding each other's turmoil while drawing strength from their collective pain. We waited and watched to see how the pieces would fall into place, but that voice that spoke to me during Ryan's younger years was looming. Something felt off.

I flew home reluctantly to deal with legal issues from the plane crash. I was swooning over my precious little niece and the short amount of time I got to spend with her, only to go home to a tiny hell on Earth. Without getting into the nitty-gritty of legal crap I had to deal with, I will simply state that the pain of grieving someone is hard enough, but stack on being petitioned by your family and having to go through the trials of the NTSB findings for four years, it was just all too much. The legal side of things stunted my healing and added another level of stress that was completely unnecessary.

Luckily after nine inundating months of legal woes and a type of stress I've never experienced, that portion of legal turmoil was over. The good part was that the family fight ceased. My immediate family and I were relieved that portion was over, but more was still to come, and that still felt defeating. The pain still overshadowed my grieving and the future pain still needed to happen before I could completely put matters to rest. For now, I took the win of overcoming this portion and moved forward.

One month later, I flew back to Idaho to spend more time with my family and the newest little bundle of joy. My Aunt joined us for a couple of weeks, and that was such a blessed time. Relaxation, laughter, and love were the main adjectives I would use to describe our time in the mountains, and bonding with my angel, my brother, and my family was precisely what I needed.

This visit ended up providing two blows I didn't see coming. The first was the day my parents drove my Aunt back to the airport. The NTSB's final conclusion document was released publicly. I wasn't going to read it at first, but as I sat on the couch, I felt I needed to know all the facts, and hopefully this would put things to rest and bring closure to this facet of the case. I opened my computer and began to read, anticipation and anxiety building as I reached the portion of the document discovering something we hadn't heard before. By this time, we knew the ultimate reason for the crash was co-pilot error, but what we didn't know were the findings of what could have occurred.

When something like a plane crash happens, your mind goes to all the horrible things your loved one suffered. Did he know this was the end, was he terrified, what were his last thoughts? You wonder if he suffered, and if he did, you pray it was milliseconds. In my case, I would have random flashes of the flames and would wake myself up with visions of the horror of those flames and Nick consumed by them. I can never forget the images I saw on TV. They were the most tragic images I have witnessed, knowing my love was trapped. You think about the team that scavenged the wreckage and found Nick's burnt body. It's grotesque to read this, but it's real. Imagine how many who suffered losses like this have to endure these thoughts while grieving forever. At that moment I read words that added a new layer of complete destruction to my world. Without quoting verbatim, it read, "The findings conclude that there could have been survivors if the door hatch and escape routes were not jammed."

I slammed my computer and screamed at the top of my lungs in pain. I screamed as if someone was hurting me, breathlessly sobbing and uncontrollable heart palpitations and despair grabbed hold of my soul. I was alone in the house, and why I didn't wait until my parents returned from the airport to read this, I will never know. It took me a solid ten minutes to stop hyperventilating and begin to calm my breathing. I thought of Nick struggling to get out of the plane and knowing he couldn't. I felt his angst and despair and fear. I screamed to God asking, "Why couldn't you have saved them. Why did Nick have to suffer through his worst nightmare?" The knife was pushed deeper as every thought and feeling I had surfaced again. The anger I experienced was red rage. But then my thoughts began to slow, and my heart paced back into rhythm, and I was able to call my cousin, who I knew would help bring me back to a rational state.

The Beauty Within Tragedy

When my cousin picked up immediately, I could tell he just read the same report. He and Nick were very close friends. Nick was one of his groomsmen. Even though I knew he read it, I asked to make sure. He said he just finished reading the report. I expressed my utter anger and sadness, and used so many choice words for how life is completely unfair. But then my cousin spoke words that shifted my entire demeanor. He stated, "Didn't the coroner's report show Nick died from blunt force trauma to the abdomen?" I immediately halted all those emotions and thought about the coroner's report. He was right! Nick died on initial impact and had no idea what followed. His demise was as quick as I would have hoped. He never knew what was coming, as it was seconds before the crash happened.

There was never a time to process or feel fear. At least I pray that was the case. He never knew of those flames. At that moment, I realized Nick wouldn't have been a survivor, and although that thought is terrible, I felt relief. I was so grateful my cousin was able to connect the dots and provide me with the words I desperately needed to hear. I will forever be thankful for that phone call, more so than he will ever know. I would never have thought that the devastating coroner's report would be my saving grace. The four months after Nick died and I received this packet in the mail, it felt like another piercing blow. Yet now, it became the rational and "thank God it happened this way" salvation.

The second blow of this trip was my eyes rejecting my contacts. After being born with cataracts and 37 years of wearing contacts, my eyes were rejecting them, and I couldn't see without them. My trip home was rescheduled, and I got to see an ophthalmologists. It was finally time to schedule a lens replacement surgery when I got home.

This was a huge pain, but after all was said and done, I could now see without contacts. Life turned into something I have never experience before! I could wake up and see clearly for the first time. Life changing! This particular event would become one that made my future life so much easier, and for some very important reasons I didn't see coming.

Acceptance Understandings

Unexpected Horror Can Be Tamed By Unexpected Things.
Just when you think the pain you're experiencing can't get worse, it does. It's almost inevitable, or at least it feels that way at times. Accepting that the next horror is possibly looming may save you from the shock of when it occurs. But in reality, we never want to live expecting the worse. Just be aware it can happen. When or if the next worse layer hits, you can shrug and say, "yup, here we go again," or you can take time to think through what this layer means. Try to postulate the reason and attribute meaning to your circumstance. Accept that the worst may not be the absolute worse, and there is probably a way to tame this new pain, even if you don't know how. The clarity of this notion may not be immediate as it was in my case, but the surprise of finally understanding why that layer had to happen will show its face. Something that initially hurt you may become the rational reason you needed to endure it. An unanswered occurrence you couldn't explain may become explainable.

The Curveballs of Life Will Keep Coming. No matter how much is on your plate, life does not stop because you are grieving. Health issues will arise, job problems, financial woes, friend turmoil, whatever the next life curveball is, figuring out how to accept it is imperative. Nothing around you stops so you can grieve peacefully; learning to understand that fact is key to focusing on how to deal with it. Your pain and grief will remain as your work through the next battle. Being able to compartmentalize and figure out how to overcome the next hurdle is challenging.

You can do it! Plain and simple, you can figure out how to refocus your mind to accept that you get to muster up more strength to cope. Our mind is powerful, and it will provide the mental awareness of how to handle the curveballs regardless of the immense pain you live with every day. Believing in yourself is the first step to understanding how to deal with external challenges as you live with internal pain.

The strength it takes to ride the rollercoaster of grief already proves that you have the power to endure hardship. Those hardships are a part of what makes life full. If we didn't have hard times, we could never appreciate good times. If we never felt pain, we could never feel love. If we never, we could never.

Lessons Learned

Drug Abuse and Mental Anguish. I will not pretend to know what it's like to battle addiction, nor will I speak on how to cope and overcome this disease. I will touch on the person that knows someone battling this disease, it's a course that can be triumphed, but also one that cannot. There are many facets of what brings a person down the path of alcohol and drug addiction. It's a personal battle they must face on their time. You can help, but you cannot force change. You can support but not retrain someone's mind.

The mental anguish, or in Ryan's case, psychological issues, plays a huge role in the healing process and stunts the addiction healing. The best advice I can provide for any family dealing with similar circumstances is to listen to what your family member wants to express. Be a sounding board and really listen to the pain they are experiencing. Provide insight and aid, but learn to cope with your internal pain if they cannot accept it. We cannot control others, but we can control how we allow issues to infiltrate our thoughts and life. Try to help, but when the help becomes so overbearing or overlooked, it's okay to focus on what heals you from this pain.

Helping Those We Love Most. There's a hundred different ways we can help another person, and that is something you will only know how to do based on your relationship with them. But on the other hand, we cannot always be the person that helps our loved ones. It's true what they say, "the closer the relationship, the harder it is for another to heed the advice given." I'm sure there is science behind why we don't always listen to our closest allies, but in my opinion, we have to allow the person struggling to take control of their journey.

You are not a fixer of all things. Not for yourself and not for others. Thinking we can solely fix everything in our own lives segregates us from understanding what human connection through communication means for longevity of life. So being able to understand when we are doing more of an injustice or not equipped to handle the situation is the time we must love that person enough to let them figure things out on their own time. This concept is for the preservation of self and the person you love. You cannot appreciate transformation if you don't personally discover it along the way. It's like giving the ending to the movie when it begins, you ruin the experience. Provide clarity, but allow for their self-discovery in order to prove to themselves why life is precious and beautiful.

Personal Pain Doesn't Overshadow Others Joy. No matter what internal anguish you are suffering, it's possible to look beyond the darkness and find joy in the happiness of others. This is true even if their joy is from something you see desperately longed for in your life. Consumable sadness is imperative to healing, but as time ticks on, you become aware of escaping those chains and letting others' joy become your own. In fact, other's joy can minimize your sadness and replace it with a real sense that life does move forward and you can handle this evolutionary change. The power of outside joy can help you heal.

Healing Tools

Self-Awareness. Channeling your self-awareness is a practice. Sometimes we struggle to be aware of ourselves, whether that's within our own life or the lives of others. Self-awareness is the conscious knowledge of one's character, feelings, motives, and desires. To become clear, your self-awareness should be a constant work in progress for your transformation from pain. It will help you lead your life with purpose, openness, and authenticity. In turn, you will gain trust from others. Obtaining trust happens when you allow your vulnerable and raw self to be seen.

By exploring ways to become more aware of yourself you discover what you need to combat problems, challenges and pain. You can also discover what you need from other relationships to meet your needs. As a result, our deficiencies are clarified, and we can work toward effective change.

According to the Harvard Business Review (HBR), they have developed five ways to cultivate and develop this practice. Some of these I have touched on already in this book are great ways to repurpose a practice you have put in place.

Meditate. This practice can be a few minutes a day in complete serenity or an hour of reflection listening to meditation apps while focusing on breathing. You can also self-reflect while doing activities such as washing dishes, gardening, or taking a walk. Meditation does not always need to be a still practice. It can be worked into your daily life. Especially if you don't enjoy doing things like laundry, you can turn that task into a time to reflect. Ask yourself questions such as:

- What am I trying to achieve?
- What am I doing that is working?
- What am I doing that is slowing me down?
- What can I do to change?

Write Down Your Key Plans and Priorities. Hopefully in your journey, you have begun to journal your emotions, you can now go back and reflect on them. Maybe those emotions have changed, and you can write new ideas of why they evolved or how you could alternate the course of your pain. The HBR states you can write down what you want to do and track your progress. I look at this as a way to set your new goals. You will have goals again; you will want to move forward, and this is a great way to work towards your future. Start with one goal, and even if you have no idea how to fulfill it, your mind will expand on its achievement, maybe as you are cleaning those annoying dishes.

Take a Psychometric Test. These are aptitude tests designed to provide clarity of your character. They're used in many facets, such as work placement, but they can open your thoughts into new realms of yourself that you may not have discovered yet. Not only can they tell you the times of the day that your brain computes information the best, but they can bring light to skill sets undiscovered. Some examples of these tests are the Meyers Briggs and the Predictive Index.

Ask Trusted Friends. Just as we conduct field research at work to gauge sales and Marketing strategies, we can conduct research on ourselves with our peers. We can guess, but we ultimately don't know how our friends perceive us. To go down this path, you much channel an open mind to accept constructive criticism. If you want to be true to who you are, being true to others means we need to reflect on a perception we may not have known others see. Write down their views and think about points you want to correct. Another tactic the HBR states is to ask your friends to call you out on behavior you have expressed you want to change. This gives you direct accountability and realization of things unseen.

Get Regular Feedback at Work. Your work colleagues see you differently from friends or family, so if they are willing, ask them to provide insight into your character. This exercise can be geared solely toward your work life or personal. Learning how we are viewed at a place we spend over 50% of our time can give you awareness of how to be a better leader or co-worker. In addition, it can provide a dimension that will further your career goals and, in turn, play into your overall self-awareness for a complete you.

You are never finished becoming self-aware. It's a lifelong practice that will continually evolve. It's the only way to reach what is known as, self-congruence, aligning how we think, feel and speak consistently.

Time is Still Your Best Friend. The constant understanding of how time is a healing mechanism needs to be enacted as a powerful tool. Too many times we put unnecessary pressure to have it all figured out right now. We feel we need to fix everything quickly to live fully. Write down a mantra such as, "Time is what I have and what I need to heal." Everything takes time. We never should act swiftly after tragedy or any life change. Be patient and figure out what is best for you at the moment, and that moment will provide the next step to long-term future goals.

The Beauty Within Tragedy

Grim Reaper Strikes Again

After returning to his family home in February, Ryan fully focused on the truest love of his life, his daughter. While I was in Idaho visiting, Ryan chose to rejoin his family and move home to Florida, where he planned to restart a beautiful life. In February of 2017, Ryan and Isabella flew home to Florida, and the thick air we were all breathing for so long suddenly thinned. We were all living under the same roof, my parents, myself, Ryan and Isabella. We never thought we would have the gift of living together as a whole family again, but it was just the thing we needed.

Ryan spent many days walking the beaches reflecting on his past and planning for his future with his baby girl. He was excited by the prospect of starting a new internet marketing business with me. As I stated before, Ryan and I shared an unbreakable bond of friendship, so the prospect of working together was exciting. We made many plans for the future, but the best part was that our entire family, extended and all, we're now living in the same town. We shared long overdue cousin time and many playdates with our treasure, Isabella. Being the first baby in the family is truly amazing! It seemed that we were all allowed to start over and create whatever lives we wanted. There was so much excitement, many bonds reformed and strengthened, and so much joy finally resumed in our hearts.

My brother had overcome most of his addiction problems, but not all. At this point, he was trying to manage and plan. Things were so much better than in past years, but he was also enduring so much internal, physical health damage. He wanted to get healthy and figure out a plan to do so. While in Idaho, he discovered he had onset cirrhosis of the liver. If he stopped drinking, it could be managed but completely stopping was hard. He slowed down and worked hard to overcome for the sake of his daughter. What we didn't know was there was so much more physical deterioration than he let on. Why he never expressed this to us is unknown, but I can guess that he didn't want us to worry or thought he could manage it by seeking professional help.

One early morning in March, I woke up so the sounds of Isabella ready to begin her day. I bounced out of bed to grab this sweet baby and have our private time. I walked by the room where Ryan was sleeping, which had French doors you could see through. Sleeping like a rock, as he normally did, we walked by and said our quiet "good morning Daddy" and went to get a bottle. Time passed on, and I walked by Ryan's room to change Isabella and go about our playtime. It wasn't uncommon for Ryan to sleep late. He had problems sleeping and would stay up watching movies into the wee hours of the morning.

A couple more hours passed, and I walked by his room again, noticing he hadn't changed positions in five hours. He was a very heavy sleeper, but now I thought it strange. Instead of walking in myself, I went to my Dad, who was now holding Isabella, and told him that Ryan hadn't moved in a long time. We walked over and opened the door. I touched his arm to shake it and awaken him, and he was freezing. "Oh my God, Dad he's freezing cold," I yelled. Dad told me to hold the baby, and he rolled Ryan over from his side when we noticed white spit up from his mouth and on his pillow. My Dad started yelling his name and performed CPR. I flew Isabella out of the room and screamed for my Mom to call 911.

My Dad did all he could to help save his son, knowing it was too late. Finally, the paramedics arrived and started their treatment. We prayed for a miracle, but shortly after they arrived, my brother was pronounced dead. The day we somehow knew would always come arrived. For a brief period we thought the anxiety of this day might have been in the past when he moved back home. Maybe life was going to change for the good completely, maybe we didn't have to be scared to get that phone call that something terrible happened to Ryan. Just as the air thinned and we took a breath of relief for the future ahead, my best friend was gone. Another person I loved with my whole heart was taken from our family.

My cousins, aunt, uncle, and one of my best friends were all at our home shortly after Ryan was pronounced dead. They were escorted around the side of the house because Ryan laid right by the front door. His body was covered by a sheet for hours. The dark clouds returned, and my family had to endure more pain. My Mom went into shock that day and my parents were forever changed. The loss of a child is such a cruel reality for a parent. We all sat in silence for a while and we cried. We were angry and left breathless with yet another tragic occurrence.

It was time for Ryan's body to be brought to the morgue. My family gathered around him as he was covered on a gurney. We held hands while my Uncle, the pastor, led us in prayer. I'm not sure exactly how he was able to muster the most perfect words to send his soul to Heaven, but he spoke eloquently, and we said goodbye. I couldn't tell you how much longer we all sat together, but I know I didn't want anyone to leave. Having our family all together, sharing shock, despair, anger, grief, and pain, somehow made it slightly bearable. Going through pain in a community sense does bring comfort. Knowing you have others who may feel the same emotion takes away the struggle to deal with pain singularly. You can rely on those that hurt as you do and share grief to heal together.

In the days and weeks that followed, our church wrapped us in warmth, our friends genuinely gave of themselves, our neighborhood embraced us, and we tried to find peace. The outpour was never more needed and appreciated. It was so heartwarming to receive cards, meals, knitted shawls, visits, hugs, and calls from my brother's friends. This time around, my pain was redirected, and a sense of strength filled my mind. I could not imagine my parents having to plan their child's funeral, so I did as much as I could to take that burden off of them. I wanted to be strong for Isabella and fill any emotional angst an 8-month old felt with the loss of her Daddy. What a bond the two of them shared, one I know she still feels today. Protecting her was my main goal.

As I look back now, I know that Nick's death prepared me for Ryan's. The time I needed to completely break and hit that pit of destruction was what gave me the strength to step up. I grieved Ryan, but almost turned the emotional valve off. I refocused my pain to help my parents and care for Isabella. I'm not exactly sure how to put into words the power that came over me. Maybe it was God giving me all the power that others gave to me during Nick's death by redirecting it to help. What I do know is that I have never truly taken the time to completely mourn my brother to the fullest. There are many reasons why that is, but I do live with times of immense pain that spring up randomly and around shadow anniversaries. I get to move forward always finding time to reflect on my grief for him.

We had one month with Ryan when he moved home before he was taken. A month forever cherished, a month so badly needed, a month that set a tone for change. I'm still amazed at how things all happen for specific reasons. I can't imagine if Ryan was still living in Idaho, and he passed. Thankfully that's a pain we will never have to endure. That decision he made to come home gave our family time together and final moments that will last a lifetime.

Acceptance Understandings

Death is Indefinite and Does Not Coincide with Your Timeline. You can be in the process of recovering from an initial tragedy, and the second one can hit at any moment. Accepting that life is never fair and does not always provide salvation after one trauma is something to let sink into your mind, do not live in anticipation.

119

Something else will happen and when it does, use the lesson learned from the past to help cope with the present. Take all the tools you used to better your heart and mind and implement them for your next challenge.

Take in Love. We are not designed to fight every battle on our own. That is why a battle takes an army, and a village is called upon to help raise children. People want to provide a safe haven of love and hope, let them. Even though the transformative battle you go through to reset a new future is yours and yours alone, the people that impact self-navigation shape how we grow. Don't turn away an ear, a gift, a meal or a hug. These acts will make your life a little less difficult. They will smooth the bumps created by pain and give a reprieve from turmoil. Accepting that others are an intricate piece to complete your puzzle is hard for some, but confronting pain and grief are more important than the time to introvert yourself. Take all the love you can get, and it's that love that will build you up better than before your pain.

Lessons Learned

Simple is Beautiful. Cherishing the happiness life provides is something we often overlook. I think back to the final dinner my cousins and I had with Ryan. We laughed so hard, told stories of the past and Ryan got to bond with my cousins in a way he probably never had before. I remember sitting back during that dinner and thinking how happy I was and how happy we all looked and felt that night. I now learn to sit back and view moments like this in a new light. One of gratefulness and appreciation that I get to have happiness and choose happiness in my life regardless of the circumstance I live through. The simple is now grand and the small moments are now large.

Healing Tools

Re-channel Pain. You can find strength when you are suffering. Doing for others and redirecting pain is powerful. Helping is healing and proves your resiliency. This tool can be controversial because professionals will say you need to solely focus on yourself, which is correct. But there will come a time when you will want to do for others again. It may, and should, start small, like sending a text to see how someone else is feeling. Perhaps a friend has a new baby, and you would like to bring over a meal, or an elderly neighbor needs her groceries picked up and delivered. These acts bring you back to a sense of normalcy and provide accomplishment that you can find strength amidst the pain. It will also make you feel good. Feeling good is not an easy task when dealing with grief and transformation, so take the time to rechannel your pain into something good for someone else. Watch as the positive endorphins release their magic back into your body.

Full Circle Coming

The Lifetime movie unfolds even further. My brother's girlfriend became pregnant with their second child in September of 2016. The rest of the family was told the news when my Aunt and I were visiting in October. By this time, their relationship was in shambles, and Ryan was already thinking about removing himself and Isabella from a very toxic environment. Ryan was naturally overjoyed with the news but scared at what this meant for his future plans. What we all knew was that Ryan had to leave, or the redundant battle of toxicity would never halt. Ryan also knew there was a possibility that the baby might not be his, but we all lived the following months thinking that was not true.

By the time Ryan moved home, his relationship, in his mind, was over. In his girlfriend's mind, that was not the case. To write the details of this journey would take us into another book. I will write that his girlfriend continued her addiction, harming her unborn child yet again in utero. Ryan was beside himself with guilt for his baby, I was enraged by her actions, and the list of emotions continued. We were worried this baby may not make it, but we kept praying.

Ryan had passed, and it was time to call and tell his girlfriend. We waited days before making this call. That might seem incredibly cruel to readers, but we were trying to process our loss and frankly we were petrified at what she might do when she heard the news. We were scared for her, the baby, and her other child she had before meeting Ryan. Finally, I sat down to call her, and when she picked up, my heart sank. I asked her if she was driving, and she said no.

Then I asked if she would please sit down, and when I said those words her trembling words were, "Robin, oh my God, what happened? Is Ryan ok?" I explained that he had passed away in his sleep, and as you can imagine, she lost her mind. After a long time of trying to catch her breath, we decided to hang up, and I promised to stay in contact with her and told her to call me whenever she liked.

A few days later we received a call from her Mom letting us know that Ryan's girlfriend had been arrested for her 4th DUI and child endangerment as her son was in the car. The first emotion I felt was disgust that she endangered her child, herself, and her unborn baby, my niece! The second emotion was sadness because I knew exactly the pain she was feeling from losing the person she loved. My relationship with her was one of constant trying. I was trying to accept her as my brother's partner and mother of his children, ltrying to accept her personal addiction journey, and trying to help in any way I could. I did it for Ryan, because I wanted them both to live a healthy life and grow together, but it became very clear that would never happen.

The girlfriend was pregnant and off to jail again. The third emotion I felt after finding this out was relief. She was the safest she could be in jail, with no substances to consume, or I hoped, but she was still taking methadone prescribed by her doctor. What was going to happen to her? What was going to happen when the baby was born? Along with her Mom, we devised a plan and made the decision that I would be the best person to take on guardianship. Since I was Isabella's legal guardian it was the right choice, and I was so thankful we came to a mutual agreement.

Ten days before the baby's birth, we found out the girlfriend had appointed Power of Attorney to her Mother to care for the baby. Shocked by this news, there was no swaying the decision with her Mother; no persuasion or logical sense seemed to matter that we agreed to my apppinted guardianship. The good news for us, we knew Power of Attorney did not grant guardianship rights to any person. Our lawyer that handled Isabella's guardianship paperwork had been in contact with us since Ryan's death. We double-checked that there were no legal ramifications to the POA and devised a new plan of our own. Since the shady working of Mother and Daughter was undenounced to us, we set the plan in motion for an Ex Parte Temporary Guardianship Petition that would come into play once the baby was born. We were going to do everything in our power to save this child from following in the steps of her Mother. This is what Ryan wanted, and I promised him I would fight to protect his children.

On June 14, 2017, my parents got the call that baby Fiona Ryan was born, happy and healthy! Within two hours, my Dad booked our flights to Boise. We packed, and my Aunt, ready with snack baggies in hand, drove us to the airport while my Mom stayed in Florida with Isabella. We arrived late that night and got situated for the next morning. We anticipated what the day would bring but had no clue what to expect.

We woke up early and headed to a lawyer's office that our lawyer recommended, and she had already informed them of our situation and arrival. We had the paperwork notarized, filed, and the petition was granted for emergency temporary guardianship within hours. We went to the hospital and immediately informed the proper personnel of the situation, and things were set in motion and caused quite a stir in the hospital. We saw the girlfriend's Mom and asked if she would come to our hotel for a meeting. We couldn't see Fiona as the girlfriend was under custody. Hours later, the meeting was held at the hotel, and things did not end up going well. The Mom stormed off back to the hospital.

The next day, the girlfriend was escorted back to jail. Even though we were allowed to see Fiona before her departure, we decided for all involved that it was best if we waited. We did have a DNA test performed during our wait to be 100% sure Fiona was Ryan's baby. By this point, we were all praying so hard that she was his, and thank you Jesus, she was! It was 6:00 pm, and we were escorted into the nursery where Fiona was placed in my arms. She was so tiny, weighing 4 lbs. 15 oz., but she was perfect. As I held this tiny miracle, I thought about how much Ryan would love to be holding his second baby girl.

The doctor came over asking questions and told us about her high bilirubin levels and that we would have to take Fiona home with a special blanket to combat the levels. She was also tested for Neonatal Abstinence Syndrome (NAS) since the girlfriend was addicted and prescribed opioids, drank alcohol etc. There is a scoring system called Finnegan's Neonatal Abstinence Scoring Scale designed with 31 items to quantify the severity of NAS and to guide treatment. It's administered every four hours, and individual NAS symptoms are weighted (numerically scoring 1–5) depending on the symptom and the severity of the symptom expressed. Infants scoring an 8 or greater are recommended to receive pharmacologic therapy. Fiona had been consistently testing at a 7 when born, and overnight would teeter between a score of 6-7.

We were told we could take her home. I immediately told the doctor that I wanted her kept through the weekend for observation. I had been researching withdrawal in newborns, and discovered that the signs Isabella were showing as a newborn were withdrawal symptoms, and she should have been tested for NAS and treated. That poor baby suffered, and we didn't put two and two together. So, this time I wasn't taking any chances and explained the scenario to the staff. They explained that it wasn't necessary based on her average score, but my insistent behavior convinced the doctor to keep Fiona. Our home was two plus hours away, so we decided to drive there and rest and get ready to bring Fiona home.

Saturday afternoon, one day after we left, I received a call from the doctor stating that Fiona had been scoring a 5-6 since Friday night and that we had to come pick her up. I pleaded with him asking them to please keep her until Monday as I knew from research signs of NAS don't always appear within the first few days of life. I was overruled and told they had to discharge her. We drove back to Boise and picked her up after I made my point blatantly clear that I do not support this release.

As we drove home, tears filled my eyes as I realized how sad it was that Ryan would never meet his daughter. A new level of pain sunk into my chest as the unfair reality of life surfaced again.

That night Fiona slept in a bassinette in my room. I was so hyper-aware of everything she was doing that I was checking her breathing every five minutes. So, I scooped her up, propped myself up so I wouldn't fall asleep, and held her in my lap all night and watched. About two hours in, I felt her body stop moving and placed my hand on her chest and my finger under her nose. She stopped breathing, and my anxiety shot through the roof. My immediate reaction was to put my hands on her arms and jolt her, slightly mind you, but enough to do something, anything.

She flinched, woke up, and began breathing again. I had never been so scared in my life. I walked around the room with her, and she fell right back to sleep. I'm not sure why I didn't wake my Dad or call the hospital, but I watched and waited, knowing if it happened again, I would make the call. She had a bottle a few hours later, and the next day we each took turns by her side. Sunday came and went, and we thought maybe things would be fine, but something still felt off. She had a checkup scheduled at the pediatrician's office Monday afternoon, so we waited to see how she would check out at the visit.

Monday mid-day Fiona started to throw up a cottage cheese substance and was having slight breathing problems. She had to catch her breath sporadically and became very restless. Her food wasn't staying down, and her skin started to look blotchy. So, we called the pediatrician and told them we were coming in early due to the symptoms. Upon arrival the doctor didn't understand why she was having these symptoms. She treated the biological mom and believed her when she said she was not taking any medications or drugs. I explained that was not the truth. The doctor prepped for a blood test, bilirubin test and began calling the hospital in our town. Mind you, this is a small town and there was not enough staff on call at the hospital to take on a patient at times.

Fiona's tests did not come back with good results, so the doctor sent us home with a promise that she would get us into the hospital as soon as she could. I realize how strange this sounds. Why didn't we just drive straight there and figure it out? She was finally calm and hadn't thrown up in two hours, so we thought wait and then go, so stupid, but we did. Upon arriving home, my Dad, being who he is, said there's no way he's sitting here and waiting. So he left for the hospital and told me to keep Fiona home and wait until we could get help.

About ten minutes after he left Fiona started throwing up and having tremors. I grabbed her diaper bag and threw anything she might need in there, and picked up the phone to call 911. Our lifelong family friends came over just at that moment, and through tears I asked them if they would drive us to the hospital. We ran out of the house, called my Dad, and headed to the ER. I'm sure as we were driving, my Dad raised hell to get us what we needed because when we arrived, they rushed to our aid and began working on Fiona.

I will never forget the image of this tiny 4lb baby on a gigantic raised gurney with a team of doctors and nurses around. Her NAS score was at a 14, and we were told they have the med vac team arriving to drive us to the airport to be airlifted back to Boise Hospital. I jumped in the ambulance, and we drove to the airport, where they loaded Fiona into the back with the paramedics by her side. I jumped in the co-pilot seat. The pilot was the nicest man and made the 40 minute flight semi-bearable. So many thoughts raced through my mind. "Please let her be okay. Please don't let this plane crash. I hate the woman that did this to her!" We touched down safely, and the next ambulance was on-site and whisked us to the ER.

The ER team was comprised of five people ready to bolt into action. After reviewing the chart, another doctor was confused about why Fiona was suffering to such an extreme. I placed my hand over the chart and directly stated that the biological mother had lied throughout her entire pregnancy, explaining she was on opioids, drinking, and still smoking. Immediately the doctor set the team in motion, and I waited.

My Dad packed up the things we needed back home to stay in Boise, not knowing how long we would be there. He arrived the next morning, and Fiona was stable and placed on a four phase morphine treatment in the NICU. Her symptoms were skin mottling, tremors, sneezing, high pitch crying, muscle tone, excessive yawning, fever, blood pressure spikes, and increased tachypnea. I sat holding her for ten hours a day, rocking in our chair, knowing she needed all the love and comfort she could get. Anxiety was my daily life, and fear of the unknown loomed. During this time, a Guardian Ad Litem was assigned to us as we still had an uphill journey ahead.

The Beauty Within Tragedy

We spent 17 days in the NICU while Fiona transitioned through the morphine phases. Finally, on the 17th day was when the doctor came in and said she could be released to go home. I thought I was dreaming when I heard the news. My Dad and I were delighted, and we rushed to get everything ready to take this precious warrior home. I have so much gratitude for the staff, as they were so caring and loving. It's here where Fiona's nickname was formed, our little Fifi.

We drove to our home and had a flight booked to fly to Florida two days later. We invited the biological grandmother to our house for a final visit, which she accepted. The next day we flew home to Florida and took a sigh of relief.

The months that followed brought celebration of Isabella's first birthday, permanent guardianship of both Isabella and Fiona, and all the fun holidays Fall and Winter bring. During this celebratory time, there was still conflict with the biological mother. After being released from jail, more lies continued as she tried to re-enter society and prove to be a worthy parent. The lies were soon exposed that she was not choosing to live a pure and clean life.

As life goes, more medical complications came my way, and I needed to have a partial hysterectomy. After a decade-long battle to conceive and the disappointing pain that caused, the physical pain prevailed and became increasingly worse. It was time to get that uterus out and move far beyond the emotion and physical pain it had caused. Even though I was happy to make this decision, you can imagine the drudged-up past that came to the surface again. Yet, it was time to go on and get it out!

I remember waking up from the procedure and almost immediately asking for Nick. I had gone through so many surgeries at this point it seemed like an old habit, but this one was different. I struggled the days before thinking the worst for some reason. I relived the trauma we went through trying to conceive and the triumphs we thought we won that were lost. He was with me every step of the way. I prayed for him to be with me and keep me safe during the surgery. I distinctly recall feeling his presence before I fell asleep in the operating room. I woke up, and after a few minutes, the nurse asked me something (now I can't remember what) and I started talking about Nick and balling. It almost felt like an anxiety attack. He was always the first person I saw when I woke up from one of these procedures, and now, he wasn't physically there.

The nurse ran to get my parents, even though no visitors were allowed during initial recovery, but thankfully, this wonderful nurse knew something wasn't quite right. I probably scared the crap out of her with my intense breakdown. As my parents came to console me, they explained to the nurse what happened to my husband. Mom and Dad approached my bedside, and I just cried and cried as they tried to soothe me. The battle was over, and I just wanted Nick to be there to share in the struggle and finality of the fight. I know he was with me the entire time I was under and when I woke up, which was a comfort. I am still grateful to know his spirit got me through that time.

Since I chose to go the traditional route for that procedure, my recovery was a six week plus duration. My parents graciously and willingly took on the care of Isabella and Fiona as I healed. For anyone who has endured a laparotomy, you understand the toll it takes and the time needed to heal. The little visits from the girls made it so much easier to rest, knowing I had to heal as fast as possible to get back to them. I felt relief my uterine journey was over, and now it was all about leading a much healthier and comfortable life.

One afternoon, my Dad woke me up to check my email. It was from my lawyer, stating that the girls' biological Mom had decided to relinquish her rights to the girls and asked if I wanted to adopt them. I shot up from a horizontal position, as fast as one could shoot up after surgery, and picked up the phone to call my lawyer. After I heard her voice on the other line, I asked if this was real, and she replied, "It is real," with great excitement in her voice! Dad, Mom and I were all on speaker, and my lawyer sounded just as shocked as we did at this amazing news. Could it be true after all this time, the dream and work dedicated to making this notion a reality came to fruition?

It had been eight months of legal communication trying to fight for these babies, to give them the life they deserved, the life my brother so desperately wanted them to have. Discovery and depositions, phone mediations, petitions, you name it, we did it, and we did it for those angels. During the time right before the deposition, my Dad and I were in his home office gathering all the information we could to make the depo a success. I remember pausing for a minute. I had been through my own depo, and it was one of the worst experiences of my life. I recalled sitting across a board room table being ripped to shreds with innuendos, the lies that were made to look true, and the questions that tore my heart into a million pieces, and I thought this is going to destroy a part of the bio Mom's soul.

I was looking down, holding my cell, and in that moment, I froze. All apps disappeared as they flew away, and the picture I have on my home screen of Ryan and me was the only thing I saw. I have had a phone freeze numerous times, but never like this; it was freaky and so cool at the same time as nothing was on the phone, literally nothing but our picture staring back at me telling me it's all going to be ok! So this is my brother in action, letting me know I was doing the right thing no matter the hurt it imposed, telling me to go forward, be strong. That deposition was for the right reasons, and Ryan reaffirmed to go at all costs. The signs are everywhere from our loved ones. We just have to be open to seeing them. It was that depo my lawyer gave to the bio Mom that had her reevaluate her life and the life of her children.

Shortly after I accepted the request for adoption, I received a call from the bio Mom. Of all the times we talked, this was by far the most real and honest. We spoke about how she knew she had to allow Isabella and Fiona to live a life with the happiness they deserved. We talked about Ryan, and the emotional journey she was on. I expressed sincere hope for her life to become what she had always dreamed. It was the best talk the two of us ever had, ending with mutual respect for the decision she made. Sadly, months later, she ended up back in jail, but that reaffirmed that her selfless act of relinquishment was the best course for all, most notably the girls.

We surprised our entire family with the news at a gathering in my parent's home. It was one of the most exciting days of my life. I had made postcard-sized cards with their pictures that read, "We are Being Adopted" and placed them under the salad plate, or in our Italian family's case, pasta plates. So when they picked them up to go to the buffet, they would see the news. My Uncle was the first to discover the card, and as soon as he did, he gave me the biggest and warmest hug. Tears of joy ran down our faces. Then, the rest of my family discovered the news, and we all just screamed, cried, and felt the overwhelming emotion that this entire story had come full circle.

The day before Fiona's 1st birthday, we walked into the courthouse to adopt my baby girls. Dressed in matching pink dresses with white polka dots, we all sat in the courtroom as my adoption lawyer told the story of how this all occured. The judge never heard a story quite like mine, and was in awe and rejoiced in granting this motion. Isabella was casing the courtroom, and Fiona sat in my lap while the story unfolded.

In her tiny, sweet, little voice, Fiona started saying, "Happy day" repeatedly. In disbelief, we all stopped to listen to her and swooned over such a miraculous moment. It was a happy day for sure, one I couldn't believe was happening, one I prayed for constantly. The ruling for adoption was complete, and in an instant my dream title becomes a reality. I was a Mom!

We celebrated for hours at a fantastic party my family threw. Happiness was an understatement. I felt pure euphoria for the first time in a very long time.

Acceptance Understandings

Accept the Battle You Were Meant to Fight. As I've shared a few times, fife never slows down because we are grieving. In fact, it shoves harshness down our throats even harder during these times. If and when something else arises that you can't possibly imagine being able to deal with, know you are a soldier of your life. You can fight through anything and triumph. Sometimes that next battle can help you heal during your present grief state. Swinging the sword to slay the next dragon proves we can move forward. We can be resilient, daring, and overcome immeasurable challenges when we believe in ourselves. Whatever problem arises, know it was meant for you specifically because you're the only one that knows how to prevail even in darkness.

Lessons Learned

Always Follow Your Gut. That tiny voice inside us saying "something is not right" is typically always right! Trusting yourself during challenging times or grief is the only way to answer the call of your own life. When you trust your intuitions, you are in line with who you are, mind, body, and spirit. That all plays into achieving self-actualization, listening to your body to become congruent with your behavior.

This lesson is simple, listening to yourself and not doubting what you feel will provide great life insight. You will clearly decipher right and wrong and trust your thoughts completely to make a sound judgment. Self-doubt inhibits us from taking risks that could positively impact our future. Having confidence in your gut voice lets,' your real voice be heard clearly and unapologetically.

Healing Tools

You Never Know How Life Heals You Until You Live It. You get to keep living even though you may want to curl into a ball and not move. The "curl into a ball" days are needed for survival and to kickstart a new motivation possibly lost. Then after those days, trust that you will live fully again if you continue to live without fear of the unknown. I had no clue if I would ever be a Mother, but tragically and unexpectedly, I was given that gift. I kept living and healed a wound I thought I would carry with me the rest of my life. Trust in yourself that you will make it and trust life to heal you, maybe unexpectedly.

"There is nothing that can happen TO you that can't also happen FOR you...if you let it."

- *Mandy Hale*

The Beauty Within Tragedy

My Beautiful Baggage

This book has taken much longer than anticipated to write. I had a very lofty goal of writing it in three months. It has now been two years since that goal was set, but I have grown and experienced so much more that was imperative to its completion.

I've toiled through my own grief gauge crying and laughing my way through the writing of this book. Reliving painful moments, but those moments needed to happen. We never stop living through pain. We only learn how to move forward with it and make it work to our advantage. The stories I told gave me another opportunity to heal. Another outlet to work through and gain perspective.

My List of Tragically Beautiful Lessons

I've learned to take the long way home and roll the windows down.

I've learned that those who judge the most are the ones that should work on themselves the most.

I've learned to let go, not only of things but of people that are toxic.

I've learned that grace can be felt in the most unexpected places and people.

I've learned that those you called family may not always stay your family.

I've learned that weakness is a sign of strength.

I've learned how to ask for help and accept it.

I've learned that you truly cannot understand someone's pain until you have experienced it exactly.

I've learned that no matter the truth, others will believe what they choose.

I've learned evil comes in unexpected forms.

I've learned that friends will choose sides and will not think to ask about another perspective.

I've learned the desire to prove yourself only matters if you're the person who needs the proof..

I've learned comfort from a stranger warms your heart more than you think it would.

I've learned that no matter the respect you give someone they may not return it.

I've learned the love you know to be true is truth.

I've learned to trust my gut.

I've learned to let my heart heal no matter the time frame.

I've learned not to care so much about things I cannot change.

I've learned that those who have always been my constant will remain that way.

I've learned that compassion comes in many forms.

I've learned that doing for others even in times of complete despair makes you smile.

I've learned that the one you loved the most will disappoint you th most.

I've learned that I do not need to be strong all the time and I do not need to be strong for everyone else.

I've learned how to be self-focused and be okay with that choice.

I've learned that an irresponsible choice may be the best choice.

I've learned that life breeds happiness, and you have to work hard to achieve it and choose it every day.

I've learned allowing myself the luxury of time to heal is priceless.

I've learned that I do not need the opinions of others unless I ask for them.

I've learned that the prayers that went unanswered and I didn't understand why, always become clear.

I've learned perfection is not the key to happiness.

I've learned what it's like to lose yourself.

I've learned that walking into the storm is the best way to get through it.

I've learned never to judge even if you don't agree or understand someone's choices or reckless actions.

I've learned that finding peace is the best way to heal.

I've learned that continuous work on yourself allows your mind to expand to enlightenment.

I've learned that taking drastic actions may sound crazy to some, will help strengthen your being.

I've learned I do not need to explain my actions.

I've learned to say, "No."

I've learned that people you thought would understand the most sometimes don't.

I've learned that work does not define your success.

I've learned to view the world in a more simplistic and beautiful light.

I've learned the life I thought I needed is not the life that needs to be.

I've learned that I will be blamed for things that have nothing to do with me because others aren't strong enough to realize that life unfolds as it should.

I've learned I will be viewed as bad even though I am good.

I've learned it's okay to verbalize every single emotion you feel.

I've learned that others will think they know everything when they really know nothing.

I've learned to remind myself that you can still be the better person no matter the pain others inflict on you.

I've learned to protect those that cannot speak for themselves.

I've learned that my relationship with God has protected me and has grown deeper.

I've learned that others will never realize the amount of pain they cause another person.

I've learned that my lost love has taught me many lessons in his absence.

I've learned what it feels like to be alone and how to live happy in those moments.

I've learned again and again that family and those you consider family are your true core and will help you stand when you cannot.

I've learned that others will use your chosen path against you.

I've learned that even if I'm the only one that knows the truth, that's okay.

I've learned the simplest of acts will be viewed as wrong.

I've learned that other's insecurities will play into your life, and then I learned how not to let them.

I've learned that you will not see eye to with everyone no matter how hard you try.

I've learned what it feels like to be unable to think or speak.

I've learned what it feels like to not care about yourself.

I've learned how to live hard today and not put pressure on the future.

I've learned that you will be tested in ways you never thought possible and continue to be tested with hard lessons all at once.

I've learned what it feels like to have your heart torn to pieces and your body hurt from pain.

The single most important lesson I've learned is that the worst time in your life can also be the most beautiful if you allow yourself to heal.

Life feels as if it came full circle. A circle is never ending, so I know there is so much more to come, but this journey has completed its loop. When it was time to start dating again, I made a few bad decisions. As in life those decisions were all made during so many life-altering changes and needed to happen just as they did. But when some of the heaviest dust cleared, the puzzle pieces started to fit together. A man named Cliff walked into my life, and even though I didn't see "it" he did. I thought of us as friends, but he pursued me to see him as anything but friends. He would show up wherever I was and always had this free spirit and easy-going vibe that was refreshing.

Cliff has an infectious passion for life and a career in MLB that he loves. He has a daughter, Samantha, and a step-daughter, Joelle, who are beautiful in every aspect of the word. We have fun together, always laughing, but also always willing and wanting to have great conversation. I met Cliff right after Ryan had passed, which typically is not the time to date anyone. But, timing is always everything, and Cliff was placed in my life exactly when I could accept a good man. He's not the bad boy (well, not anymore from what I have learned), but he definitely doesn't lack confidence. He's the guy that listens, supports, and loves fully. He's not embarrassed to be vulnerable or aware of his feelings. One day, as if a light turned on, I asked one of my best friends (who was friends with him prior to our meeting) if I should date Cliff? She said, "He would be the guy you should date. He would protect you and be the good man you deserve, always doting and supportive."

Well, the rest is history he won me over. If you ever watched Sex and the City and I was Charlotte, I describe him as my Harry. He's the good man you hope to find in life, the one that puts your feelings before his own. He supports me in a way I have never experienced from another partner. He accepts all of my Italian outbursts and imperfections (even finds them attractive). He lives to make me happy, but most importantly, he is delicate with my journey. I met him just as I was coming into my Motherhood role with Isabella, grieving my brother and amid legal drama from the plane crash. As most of that would have been looked upon by other men as major baggage, he wanted to be a part of my life.

Being with someone that lives with grief is not an easy endeavor. It takes patience, understanding, and self-confidence. I dated a guy that was intimidated by my late husband. I couldn't speak of him without a snide comment or a self-loathing attitude. Cliff has done nothing but celebrate the life I had with Nick, listen as I dealt with enormous grief, and held me as I cried through pain. He took on the role of being a Father figure to Isabella, and when I flew to Idaho to save Fiona, his excitement for me bringing home another baby was nothing short of amazing. I know Nick and Ryan brought Cliff to me, giving signs along the way to ensure I knew this was right and they had my back, as they still do.

We now share a beautiful life and home together with four amazing children. Our challenges are ones shared by all modern families, growing kids, and handling life's obstacles. We are also truly blessed to have a wonderful relationship with Cliff's ex-wife, living life as one big blessed family.

I now reflect on how I was given everything I ever wanted, but these gifts were given in a completely different way than what I ever expected.

Even though I lost Showboat, I learned how to speak hard truths even if I left myself open to negative responses. I understand that we can't always have a conclusion to a story, and I have to accept and be comfortable with that fact.

Even though I lost my unborn children, I learned that a defined IVF plan between a husband and wife is imperative for self-sanctity. I learned that no one gets to define the importance of my babies' losses because of the time they spent in utero.

Even though I lost Nick, I learned that God always shelters you a little bit from such horror. I learned why we had to separate and how two people can find their way back to one another. I learned how evil exists in the most familiar and comfortable places. I learned that no matter the truth, it won't be heard or accepted, but my truth is all that matters. I learned why I never had children with my husband.

The Beauty Within Tragedy

Even though I lost my brother, I learned that you cannot save a sibling from their demons. I learned that everything he did set his children up for the life he wanted them to have. I learned how one death can help you heal through another. Though I did not learn this, I was reminded how grateful I am to have had such a close bond with my brother that was never taken for granted. I learned that my biggest dream can come from a horrible situation.

With all these lessons, the biggest one I learned is that beauty lies in every aspect of our lives, even if we can't possibly understand that during times of tragedy. All my tragedies led me to a life of peace and transformation. I sit here today with all legal issues pertaining to the plane crash resolved. I have closure with my Mother and Sister-in-law. I have two beautiful children that make me swoom when I hear them call me Mommy.

I live in a new town surrounded by my loving family. My friends are the tribe that sticks by me no matter what happens. I celebrate EVERYTHING regardless of its simplicity. I understand my grief will come and go, and I learn how to deal with each phase in different ways. Things that use to complicate my mind are minimalized by the fact that I know I can overcome anything. I know that whatever plagues me now will not be the same burden in time. I grow every day, knowing I will never master grief, but I understand that I can change how it affects my life.

"We can either make ourselves miserable or we can make ourselves strong. The amount of work is the same." – **Carlos Castaneda**

The Beauty Within Tragedy

Tragedy is what we make of it. Are you going to let your circumstance consume your mind, body, and soul for the rest of your time on Earth? Or are you going to decide to make that tragedy mean something more than what it is in your life right now? If you choose the latter, that is where you will find the beauty within tragedy. Not only will the pain transform your thoughts positively, but life will drop answers of why your path led up to the occurrence and how it will shape all others that follow.

We are resilient as humans, and we learn to adjust to a person's absence. Loss creates holes in our lives that can never be replaced, but most times losses create discoveries. In some cases, a loss can give way to an unanswered prayer or even a dream you thought was lost. The end of something helps you find new opportunities and beliefs in things you didn't know were possible. There's pain that uses you, and then there's pain you use. The pain you use will diminish the darkness and explode color back into your life, brighter than it was before.

It's creeping up on 15 years since I lost Showboat, 10 years since I lost my first child, 5 years since I lost Nick and 4 years since I lost my brother. In total, since I was 22 years old, I have lost 15 family members (unborn children included). That's heartbreaking when you think in totality, yet each of those losses defined a part of me and how I handle and nurture my life. Each loss made me appreciate something I might not have before like rethinking how to handle situations differently, and helped me to train my voice to be heard. Loss in life is inevitable. But the power we put behind loss to give it a different meaning, turn it into a gift or paint a pretty picture from it is the beauty within tragedy.

The End...for now.

About the Author

Robin Gargano is a woman with a story, a gorgeous, messy story. She wants to share her tragedies and the beauty that was brought into her life because of these circumstances. Being able to serve others through life experiences is a gift we offer to the world and that is exactly what Robin chose to do with her new life.

As a former entrepreneur in the Marketing/Event space she now dedicates her life to showing the world how bad crap happens for us and not to us. Robin is a Resiliency Coach, speaker, author among other titles that are yet to be discovered. She is also a widow, a Mother, a daughter, a sister and a life spouse to a wonderful man.

Robin's mission is to provide awareness of individual suffering and empower people to use that pain as a catalyst to new-found gifts and beauty.

She lives in Palm Beach Gardens, Fl and is a graduate of Rollins College.

Bibliography

Ronald Knapp. Beyond Endurance, 2nd ed. (Bloomington, IN: Author House 2005) 43

Marianne Williamson. Tears To Triumph (Harper One/Harper Collins Publishing)

Doug Manning, The Journey of Grief (In-Sight Books)

Made in the USA
Las Vegas, NV
11 September 2021

30066666R00083